# Money and Finances

## ISSUES

## Volume 180

*Series Editor*

*Lisa Firth*

*Independence*

Educational Publishers
Cambridge

First published by Independence
The Studio, High Green
Great Shelford
Cambridge CB22 5EG
England

© Independence 2009

**British Library Cataloguing in Publication Data**
Money and Finances — (Issues; v. 180)
1. Teenagers — Great Britain — Finance, Personal 2. Young adults —
Great Britain — Finance, Personal 3. Finance, Personal 4. Debt
I. Series II. Firth, Lisa
332'.024055'0941-dc22

ISBN-13: 978 1 86168 504 9

**Printed in Great Britain**
MWL Print Group Ltd

**Cover**
The illustration on the front cover is by
Simon Kneebone.

# CONTENTS

# Useful information for readers

Dear Reader,

### *Issues: Money and Finances*

The global financial crisis has forced many of us to reassess how we handle our finances, with many people looking to improve their financial literacy as they navigate their way through a recession for the first time. This book examines issues including spending and saving, types of bank account, using credit and dealing with debt. There is also a chapter dedicated to young people's money, including student finances, planning for the future and budgeting.

### The purpose of *Issues*

**Money and Finances** is the one hundred and eightieth volume in the **Issues** series. The aim of this series is to offer up-to-date information about important issues in our world. Whether you are a regular reader or new to the series, we do hope you find this book a useful overview of the many and complex issues involved in the topic.

Titles in the **Issues** series are resource books designed to be of especial use to those undertaking project work or requiring an overview of facts, opinions and information on a particular subject, particularly as a prelude to undertaking their own research.

The information in this book is not from a single author, publication or organisation; the value of this unique series lies in the fact that it presents information from a wide variety of sources, including:

⇨ Government reports and statistics
⇨ Newspaper articles and features
⇨ Information from think-tanks and policy institutes
⇨ Magazine features and surveys
⇨ Website material
⇨ Literature from lobby groups and charitable organisations.*

### Critical evaluation

Because the information reprinted here is from a number of different sources, readers should bear in mind the origin of the text and whether the source is likely to have a particular bias or agenda when presenting information (just as they would if undertaking their own research). It is hoped that, as you read about the many aspects of the issues explored in this book, you will critically evaluate the information presented. It is important that you decide whether you are being presented with facts or opinions. Does the writer give a biased or an unbiased report? If an opinion is being expressed, do you agree with the writer?

**Money and Finances** offers a useful starting point for those who need convenient access to information about the many issues involved. However, it is only a starting point. Following each article is a URL to the relevant organisation's website, which you may wish to visit for further information.

Kind regards,

*[signature]*

Lisa Firth
Editor, **Issues** series

*\* Please note that Independence Publishers has no political affiliations or opinions on the topics covered in the **Issues** series, and any views quoted in this book are not necessarily those of the publisher or its staff.*

---

## ISSUES TODAY
### A RESOURCE FOR KEY STAGE 3

Younger readers can also benefit from the thorough editorial process which characterises the **Issues** series with our resource books for 11-to 14-year-old students, **Issues Today**. In addition to containing information from a wide range of sources, rewritten with this age group in mind, **Issues Today** titles also feature comprehensive glossaries, an accessible and attractive layout and handy tasks and assignments which can be used in class, for homework or as a revision aid. In addition, these titles are fully photocopiable. For more information, please visit our website (www.independence. co.uk).

# The global financial crisis

## Information from the World Bank

The current financial crisis started with the collapse of several of the world's largest financial institutions, and has since turned into a global economic crisis. Countries around the world, rich and poor, are feeling its impact in all sectors.

The economic crisis is severely affecting many areas of people's lives and livelihoods, including employment, food prices, interest rates and the money people earn abroad and send back home. Governments in the world's wealthiest nations are trying to weather the storm through large-scale economic stimulus packages for their economies. The IMF has called this the most severe recession since World War II, and has predicted that the global economy will shrink by 1.3% in 2009.

According to the IMF, the problem grew out of a false sense of security stemming from a long period of high growth, low interest rates and volatility. Bad policy also played a huge role, especially in three areas:

⇨ Financial regulation – which was not equipped to see existing risks and flaws;

⇨ Macroeconomic policies – which did not take into account the build-up of risks in the financial system and in housing markets;

⇨ Global governance – lack of co-operation among experts and senior policy makers got in the way of detecting early warning signs; there is a pressing need for sustainable and inclusive globalisation.

> **The current financial crisis started with the collapse of several of the world's largest financial institutions, and has since turned into a global economic crisis**

### How is the crisis affecting the fight against poverty?

Though it began in rich countries, the crisis is hitting developing countries hard. As a result of the food and financial crises, the pace of poverty reduction has slowed, threatening the first Millennium Development Goal (MDG) of halving extreme poverty by 2015. The overall toll of the economic downturn has been far-reaching:

⇨ Remittances that workers send home to their families are projected to fall to $290 billion in 2009, as opposed to $305 billion last year;

### Think about it

'In London, Washington and Paris, people talk of bonuses or no bonuses. In parts of Africa, South Asia and Latin America, the struggle is for food or no food. Developing countries and peoples are endangered by today's crisis. But they can also be a key part of the solution.'
*World Bank President Robert Zoellick*

⇨ 2009 GDP growth in developing countries is expected to fall to 4.5% from 7.9% in 2007;

⇨ As many as 90 million more people could be trapped in extreme poverty – living on less than $1.25 a day;

⇨ The number of chronically hungry people is expected to climb to over one billion in 2009;

⇨ If the crisis persists, a total of 1.4 to 2.8 million babies may die per year between 2009 to 2015;

⇨ Global trade is forecast to shrink in 2009 for the first time since 1982.

### What is being done?

World leaders and policymakers have recognised the global nature of the problem and the fact that it therefore requires a global solution, with all countries playing a part.

At its April 2009 summit, the G20 agreed to provide for $100 billion of extra lending through the various Multilateral Development Banks (MDBs).

The World Bank has proposed that each developed country pledge at least 0.7% of its economic stimulus package to a global vulnerability fund to help developing countries.

For its part, the Bank is focusing on three priority areas: Safety net programmes to protect the most vulnerable; maintaining investments in infrastructure; support for small and medium-size enterprises and microfinance.

---

**Though it began in rich countries, the crisis is hitting developing countries hard**

---

While the responsibility for restoring global growth lies largely with rich countries, emerging and developing countries have an important part to play in improving their growth outlook, maintaining macroeconomic stability, and strengthening the international financial system.

### What can I do?

Stay optimistic! It's not easy when all the news is so unpleasant, but the important thing is to learn some lessons from the situation to prevent it from happening again, and to help improve things.

One basic lesson from the economic crisis is that in today's world, flawed financial systems can have huge macroeconomic consequences. So, these flaws need to be understood and tackled as best possible. On an individual level, this begins with trying to understand the issues and staying up-to-date on what's going on.

It's also important to brush up on financial literacy: learning to be savvy on money matters, to save, and to spend wisely. Most of us think we need far more than we actually do, so it's a good idea to sit back and think about what we really do need, and how much of what we have (or think we should have) is superfluous.

You can also donate to development projects through websites like Kiva.org or GlobalGiving.
*4 June 2009*

⇨ The above information is reprinted with kind permission from the International Bank for Reconstruction and Development, the World Bank. Visit http://youthink.worldbank.org for more information.

# Understanding the recession

---

**You've probably heard the term 'credit crunch' bandied about in recent months, but any idea what it means? TheSite.org goes in search of an explanation of what a recession is, and how you could be affected**

### What is a recession?

A recession is defined as a reduction in a country's entire income and output (known as a Gross Domestic Product or GDP) over at least six months. This is caused by people spending less, businesses making less and banks being more reluctant to give people loans.

Recessions generally start because of a loss of confidence in the financial system. People hold on to the money that they have, rather than spend it, and that means there is less money in circulation.

It's hard to predict how long a recession will last. The last UK recession, from 1990 to 1992, was followed by a long period of economic growth right up to 2008.

### Current crunch crisis

The current recession has come about for many reasons, but mostly because of worries about the banking system.

### By Anthony Burt

UK and American banks took huge risks with their lending and investments and when things started to go sour, debts couldn't be repaid. One of the main causes of this are subprime mortgages, where banks lend to people who are considered less likely to be able to pay them back.

The credit crunch began in the UK in August 2007, when it was revealed that Northern Rock had applied to the Bank of England seeking emergency funding

When large numbers of mortgage-payers miss their repayments, the banks lose money. With less money available, they can't lend to businesses, meaning less investment and reducing the potential to make a profit. With less chance to make money, fewer people want to invest in companies, and this caused the value of the stock market to fall, or 'crash'.

---

**A recession is defined as a reduction in a country's entire income and output (known as a Gross Domestic Product or GDP) over at least six months**

---

World governments had to act fast to save the financial system. They are trying to get people to start spending, by making billions of pounds available and trying to remove bad debts. It's still too early to say how effective this action will be.

### The highs and lows

Recessions are a time of uncertainty and concern. These are some of the ways you could be affected:

⇨ Your job could be at risk, and you may find it difficult to get work.

⇨ It's harder to get a loan or credit cards, and banks will start calling loans in quicker.

---

**While some prices might be cut during a recession, others could rise as companies try to make money where they can**

---

⇨ The property market seizes up, and that makes it difficult if you are looking to buy or sell.

⇨ More people have mental health problems as they cope with rising debts, unemployment and housing problems.

⇨ 'When they first started talking about the recession I didn't think it would really affect me. Then the attendance dropped massively at the club I worked at,' says John from London. 'As a recent graduate every permanent job I've had I've lost because of

the good old last one in, first one out rule.'

There are a few upsides:

⇨ Some shops lower prices and put on more sales, so you'll bag yourself a bargain.

⇨ You'll stay in to watch more DVDs and find new ways to socialise with your friends.

⇨ You may have less money to spend and feel that life is duller, but in the meantime you'll discover plenty of activities that won't stretch your wallet.

⇨ 'One definite upside of the recession for me is that the car has been cheaper to run,' says Ben from North Wales. 'Over the summer, it would cost over £40 to fill my car, it now costs about £32 for a full tank.'

### Is my job safe?

With less money going around the system, there are fewer jobs available. Some sectors are seen as more secure. Working in the public sector (e.g. for the council, in teaching, the NHS or the police) are regarded the least at risk. Other services such as the IT industry, HR and energy and fuel companies are seen as fairly safe.

And a recession is often seen as a good time for entrepreneurs and new entrants to the market, so if you've ever wanted to run your own business, now could be the time to give it a go.

### Tightening the money belt

While some prices might be cut during a recession, others could rise as companies try to make money where

they can. But there are hardship loans if you're at university, and benefits if you're on low income that can help. You can also help yourself by doing the following:

⇨ Don't ignore people you owe money to (creditors). Get help with debt.

⇨ If you have debts, there are some you should pay first before others, such as mortgage or rent debts. If you don't pay these, you could lose your home. Debt advisers can help you plan your budget and pay your priority debts first.

⇨ Download a budget form and see if you can save money on bills, food and travel. Also check if you're claiming all you're entitled to, such as housing and child benefit.

⇨ You may be able to claim help with education costs and even get a grant to help you pay for things like fitting home insulation to cut your fuel bills.

⇨ Your gas and electricity supplier may be able to help you too if you have fuel debts.

⇨ If you are in work, you might get Working Tax Credit even if you don't have children. If you have children, are you claiming Child Tax Credit?

⇨ If you lose your job, go to your local Jobcentre Plus office and start claiming benefits such as Jobseeker's Allowance.

⇨ The above information is reprinted with kind permission from TheSite. Visit www.thesite.org for more.

© TheSite

# How the credit crunch began

## Information from Which?

The 'credit crunch' has its roots in the long-term problems which developed in the American mortgage market in recent years.

Defaults on loans made to high-risk US home buyers – known as sub-prime loans – hit the US housing and banking sectors hard in summer 2007.

To further compound this problem, banks became less willing to lend to each other on a global scale as fears mounted. These fears were largely over who held those loans and how big the losses associated with them would be. This forced the European Central Bank to inject more than Euro200 billion into the European money markets in the space of three days in August 2007.

### How Northern Rock set the ball rolling in the UK

The credit crunch hit the UK in August 2007, with the full force of the impact felt when it was revealed that Northern Rock had applied to the Bank of England seeking emergency funding. This was exposed on Thursday 13 September 2007.

The bank was forced to look to the Bank of England for support because it had struggled to raise money to finance its lending to people in the form of home loans.

While banks generally raise their lending money (used for mortgages) from customers putting their money into savings accounts, Northern Rock had been raising most of its money by borrowing from other banks and institutions. This left it more vulnerable than its rivals due to the slowdown in inter-bank lending.

### A run on the bank

Northern Rock's share price dropped once the news broke, with people starting to panic and take out cash from savings accounts. Long queues formed outside branches as news reports of the crisis fuelled further alarm.

The government stepped in to initially guarantee that savers' money would be safe, and eventually in February 2008 took the decision to nationalise the bank after private bidders failed to secure a takeover.

### Credit crunch dominoes

Northern Rock wasn't the last high street name to get into financial trouble in the months that followed. HBOS, parent company of Halifax and Bank of Scotland, was taken over by Lloyds TSB (now known as the Lloyds Banking Group), the Icelandic Landsbanki group collapsed, while Bradford and Bingley was nationalised and its savings arm sold to Spanish banking giant Santander.

And it isn't just banks that have fallen on hard times, with many chains disappearing from the British high street. High-profile, well-established names such as Woolworths, MFI and Zavvi have all closed down, with Fishworks, Whittard of Chelsea and Waterford Wedgwood also facing closure or being bought out.

The Bank of England base rate, as high as 5.75% in July 2007, has been slashed over the following 18 months, hitting just 0.5% in March 2009.

➪ The information on this page is reprinted with kind permission from Which? Limited. Visit www.which.co.uk for more information on this and other related topics.

© Which? Limited

---

# The recession in numbers

The figures below show just some of the dramatic changes that have taken place since April 2008. Figures correct at 6 April 2009.

*Bank of England base rate*
A year ago: 5%
Now: 0.5%

*Average UK house price*
A year ago: £179,110
Now: £150,946
(Source: Nationwide)

*Highest instant-access Best Buy savings rate*
A year ago: 6.26%
Now: 3%

*Financial Services Compensation Scheme limit*
A year ago: £35,000
Now: £50,000

*Average credit card rate*
A year ago: 16.1%
Now: 16.7%

*Average personal loan rate for £5,000 over three years*
A year ago: 9.74%
Now: 12.41%

© Which? Limited

# How to spot the end of a recession

### Is it possible to glimpse, through the financial doom and gloom, the tell-tale glimmers of economic recovery?

### Full price

If you can remember what that is. No longer will the January sales last until Easter, and the summer sales until Christmas, and gone will be the days of those lovely emails: a two-for-one voucher at your favourite restaurant. An economic upturn will mean no discounts, making shopping slightly less fun.

### Petrol prices

During a recession, there is often comfort to be taken in falling petrol prices. When they begin to rise, the slump may be starting to lift.

### Housing market

The housing market is a great indicator of what's going on in the economy. In the recession, the amount of mortgages that were approved stood a dismal 50% off the year before. Once you start seeing more 'For Sale' boards you'll know things are on the up.

### Holidays to Europe

The recent recession was characterised by a weak pound. Keen to avoid costly euroland, UK tourists opted for discount holidays further afield in order to avoid the euro – or staying in the UK. The average family holiday to Spain was costing on average £200 more than previous years.

So long-haul destinations became increasingly popular when holidaymakers could secure cheap flights, as they could spend less when they got there.

### Interest rates increase

The recently low interest rates might seem like a great idea for those looking to borrow, but they are a clear sign of a poor economy. Once consumers start spending again the Government needs to tighten the reins and rates will rise.

### Newspaper headlines

No news is good news isn't it? No, good news is in fact not news at all, so once the economy improves you can expect the newspapers to find a new fad to focus on for the next 18 months. What credit crunch?

### New car registrations

Falling car sales can be an indication that the economy is flagging. The recent recession saw car sales hit a brick wall and car makers struggled to stay afloat. When the car makers start enjoying better times, the end of the recession may be in sight.

### You'll have a conversation that doesn't involve the words 'credit' or 'crunch'...

...unless you're pointing out that it's easier to get credit or talking about your new favourite cereal anyway.

### Brightly dressed people

Noticing a lot of grey and black on the way to work in the mornings? Apparently a recession can be the reason we're no longer buying bold colours. Asda reported that sales of coloured tights were down 52% and sales of black tights were up 35% during the recent recession, and men bought more boring white shirts than ever before with sales up 29%.

## The recent recession was characterised by a weak pound

### Unemployment will fall

In lean times companies attempt to save money wherever possible. When they start hiring again, things may be about to turn.

*Latest update by Holly Black, April 2009*

⇨ The above information is reprinted with kind permission from This is Money. Visit www.thisismoney.co.uk for more information.

# Cost of living

## Minimum cost of living rising at twice the rate of inflation

A report released today (1 July) finds that the minimum cost of living, set by members of the public, is rising at twice the rate of inflation, making it harder to live on a low income this year than last year. A minimum income standard for Britain in 2009 calculates the income needed to afford a minimum socially acceptable standard of living in Britain. Items that make up a large part of a minimum budget, such as food, have risen sharply in price. Some items that have got cheaper, such as paying a mortgage and running a car, are not part of a minimum budget.

---

**Items that make up a large part of a minimum budget, such as food, have risen sharply in price**

---

A minimum income standard for Britain, published by the Joseph Rowntree Foundation, was first calculated in 2008. It is based on what members of the public thought people needed to achieve a socially acceptable standard of living. A year later, and in changing economic circumstances,

**JOSEPH ROWNTREE FOUNDATION**

the standard has been updated. This year's report calculates that:

⇨ A single adult with no children now needs to earn at least £13,900 a year before tax to reach the minimum standard. This is a £500 rise from 2008; nearly half of this extra income is needed for the rising cost of food.

⇨ About one in four people are living below the minimum income standard for Britain, and this is increasing as unemployment rises.

⇨ The minimum cost of living has risen by 5%, contrasting with official inflation figures of 2.5% (CPI) and –1% (RPI). A low-paid worker whose earnings were linked to the retail prices index could be 6% worse off this year, relative to the minimum cost of living.

⇨ Job loss can leave you with less than half the income that you actually need to live according to the minimum income standard for Britain.

The original focus groups believed that a car was not an essential item for everyone in Britain, and so it is not part of a minimum acceptable budget. However, while the cost of running a car has gone down this year, the cost of public transport has gone up.

Co-author Donald Hirsch, from the Centre for Research in Social Policy at Loughborough University, said: 'In tough economic times, a growing number of people will ask themselves whether they have enough income to afford a minimum acceptable standard of living. Many fall out of work. More find it hard to make ends meet. People who have taken for granted a given standard of living suddenly have their expectations shattered. In such circumstances, a benchmark like the minimum income standard for Britain can help society to keep sight of what levels of income it finds unacceptable.'

An online calculator is available for people to check whether their income meets the minimum standard for Britain at www.minimumincome.org.uk
*1 July 2009*

⇨ Press release from the Joseph Rowntree Foundation. Visit www.jrf.org.uk for more information.
*© Joseph Rowntree Foundation*

# Families cut spending by largest amount in decades

## Families reined in their spending by the sharpest rate in three decades to cope with the recession, official figures have shown

Household expenditure fell by one per cent – the biggest fall since 1980 – as families cut down on shopping trips and saved more to see out the downturn.

The figures for the last quarter of 2008 were contained in an Office for National Statistics report yesterday that painted a bleak picture of the British economy.

### Families who racked up unsupportable debts during the boom have learned their lesson and are now saving more

Hotels and restaurants suffered as cash-strapped Britons reduced spending on luxuries, helping push the country's gross domestic product (GDP) down 1.6 per cent, even lower than previously predicted.

But the revised figures also indicated that families who racked up unsupportable debts during the boom have learned their lesson and are now saving more.

The so-called savings ratio – which measures the amount of disposable income that is put away as savings or investment – climbed to the highest level in three years.

Families put away 4.8 per cent of their spare money into savings and investments in the last three months of last year, up from 1.7 per cent in the preceding quarter, the ONS said.

Households actually repaid £900 million more than they borrowed in the final three months of last year –

**By Harry Wallop**
**Consumer Affairs Editor**

the first time this has happened since the beginning of 2001.

While economists cheered the improved savings ratio as a sign that debt-ridden Britain was finally starting to tighten its belt, many savers have found they have increasingly few options for where to put their money.

With the Bank of England cutting interest rates to an all-time low of 0.5 per cent, there are now just a small handful of savings accounts that pay more than two per cent.

The stock market, despite its volatile performance over the last year, is starting to attract a small number of private investors once again.

The Investment Management Association, the trade body that monitors Individual Savings Account (ISA) sales, said more people were buying stock market ISAs in the last two months than selling them, for the first time since April last year.

Though the FTSE 100 index of leading shares has fallen from 6,376 last summer to well below 4,000, many private investors believe that this fall represents a buying opportunity.

Those active investors who said they intended to buy more shares, said they were doing so because of falls in the market and poor rates of return on traditional savings accounts.

Yesterday the ONS revised its figures for how poorly the economy had performed during the final quarter of last year, saying GDP had actually contracted by 1.6 per cent rather than 1.5 per cent.

Manufacturing and construction output both fell by 4.9 per cent, the steepest declines since 1975 and 1980, respectively.

*28 March 2009*

© *Telegraph Media Group Limited (2009)*

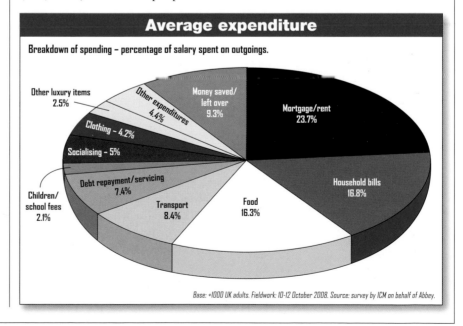

### Average expenditure

Breakdown of spending – percentage of salary spent on outgoings.

- Other luxury items 2.5%
- Other expenditures 4.4%
- Money saved/left over 9.3%
- Mortgage/rent 23.7%
- Clothing – 4.2%
- Socialising – 5%
- Debt repayment/servicing 7.4%
- Children/school fees 2.1%
- Transport 8.4%
- Food 16.3%
- Household bills 16.8%

Base: +1000 UK adults. Fieldwork: 10-12 October 2008. Source: survey by ICM on behalf of Abbey.

# It pays to save

## New report confirms benefits of saving

**M**ost people who save for their future can expect to benefit from saving under the Government's pension reform, according to research published today by the Department for Work and Pensions.

The report, *Saving for Retirement: Implications of Pensions Reforms on Financial Incentives to Save for Retirement* shows that, given reasonable assumptions about the future, most people can expect to be better off in retirement by saving, with the majority getting back more than double what they save.

Minister for Pensions and the Ageing Society Rosie Winterton said:

'This report makes clear that most people can expect their savings to make them better off in retirement.

'Rather than putting your money under a mattress, sensible saving is about making your money work harder for you, whether it is in a pension or in other ways.

'Even after inflation, virtually everyone can expect to get back more than they put away.

'The research confirms that we are absolutely right in moving forward with the recommendations of the Turner Commission and the decision to introduce auto-enrolment in 2012.'

The report looked at the impact on those making savings into a defined contribution pension after 2012 with an employer contribution. The results of the modelling were that:

⇨ Over 70% of savers can expect to get back more than twice what they put in, even after taking inflation into account;

⇨ For over 95% the expected improvement is greater than the cost of their contributions, even after taking inflation into account;

⇨ There is no readily-identifiable group in the working age population whose members cannot, on average, expect to gain back more than they put in to a pension.

The report confirms the recommendations of the Turner Commission and the decision to introduce auto-enrolment in 2012, as part of the Government's pension reform. Although there are some risks inherent in saving, the report argues that the risk of under-saving and under-providing for retirement is far greater.

Auto-enrolment and Personal Accounts will mean that millions of people will benefit, many of whom will be getting access to an employer contribution for the first time. This key element of the Turner Commission formed the core of the 2008 Pension Act.

### Notes

**1** The report, *Saving for Retirement: Implications of Pensions Reforms on Financial Incentives to Save for Retirement* is available on the DWP website at http://research.dwp.gov.uk/asd/asd5/report_abstracts/rr_abstracts/rra_558.asp

**2** From 2012 employees will automatically be enrolled into their employer's pension scheme. For employees working for an employer that does not have an occupational scheme, they will be enrolled into a personal account. For more information on personal accounts visit the Personal Accounts Delivery Authority at http://www.padeliveryauthority.org.uk

*5 February 2009*

⇨ Information from the Department for Work and Pensions. Visit www.dwp.gov.uk for more.

*© Crown copyright*

# No pension plans for 40%

## By Patrick Collinson

**F**our out of ten people in Britain have no pension provision whatsoever, according to a survey published today, as fears grow that an entire generation of workers faces poverty in retirement.

The survey, conducted for the *Guardian*'s *Money* supplement by pension provider Aegon, reveals 40% of 30 to 65 year olds will rely solely on the state pension – currently £95.25 a week. It also found those who are paying into a pension have typically accumulated less than £50,000, which at current projections will give them an income of just £60 a week.

The recession and falling stockmarkets are biting hard into pensions. After the closure of many final-salary-based schemes, companies are reducing contributions into 'money purchase' schemes. This week, insurance broker Aon cut contributions for most of its UK workforce, and Aviva axed its free pension for almost 16,000 UK staff and told final salary members they must double their contributions.

Most final-salary pension schemes are now in deficit. The Pension Protection Fund estimates 91% of schemes have a shortfall. Meanwhile, money-purchase schemes have dramatically fallen in value. Figures this week indicate that since October 2007 they have lost nearly a third of total assets. Pension providers say workers must put more aside. Rachel Vahey, of Aegon, said: 'People know they should save more, but they feel they just don't have any spare money to set aside.'

The government is pinning its hopes on auto-enrolment into pension schemes, which comes into force in 2012. This means every employer will have to automatically enrol every worker into a pension scheme and pay a contribution for them.

*11 April 2009*

*© Guardian News & Media Ltd 2009*

# Debt facts and figures

## Information from Credit Action

### Total UK personal debt

Total UK personal debt at the end of June 2009 stood at £1,458bn. This has slowed further to 1.2% in the last 12 months which equates to an increase of ~£14.35bn (the increase was ~£116bn in January 2008).

Total secured lending on dwellings at the end of June 2009 stood at £1,227bn. The twelve-month growth rate fell further, by 0.2 percentage points to 1.1%.

Total consumer credit lending to individuals at the end of June 2009 was £231bn. The annual growth rate of consumer credit continued to fall, to 1.9%.

---

### Total UK personal debt at the end of June 2009 stood at £1,458bn

---

Total lending in June 2009 grew by £0.4bn; secured lending grew by £0.3bn in the month; consumer credit lending grew by £0.1bn (total lending in January 2008 grew by £8.4bn).

Average household debt in the UK is ~£9,240 (excluding mortgages). This figure increases to £21,480 if the average is based on the number of households who actually have some form of unsecured loan.

Average household debt in the UK is ~£58,320 (including mortgages).

If you add to this the 2009 budget figure for public sector net debt (PSND) expected in 2013-14 then this figure rises to £116,160 per household.

Average owed by every UK adult is ~£30,460 (including mortgages). This is 133% of average earnings.

Average outstanding mortgage for the 11.1m households who currently have mortgages now stands at ~£110,550.

Britain's interest repayments on personal debt were £66.3bn in the last 12 months. The average interest paid by each household on their total debt is approximately £2,650 each year.

Average consumer borrowing via credit cards, motor and retail finance deals, overdrafts and unsecured personal loans has risen to £4,825 per average UK adult at the end of June 2009.

During June 2009 Britain's personal debt increased by ~£1 million every 108 minutes. In January 2008 Britain's personal debt increased by ~£1 million every 5.3 minutes.

### Today in the UK:

⇨ The average household debt will increase by £0.53 today (a decrease from £11.11 a day in January 2008).

⇨ 331 people today will be declared insolvent or bankrupt. KPMG estimate this will increase to 411 people a day throughout 2009 or one person becoming bankrupt or entering into an Individual Voluntary Arrangement (IVA) every 3.5 minutes.

⇨ In the last 12 months consumers saved an average of £2.96 every day.

⇨ 2,324 Consumer County Court Judgements (CCJs) were issued every day in the last three months of 2008.

⇨ 142 properties were repossessed every day during the last three months to end March 2009. The Council of Mortgage lenders estimates this will increase to approximately 178 a day throughout 2009.

⇨ Unemployment increased by 3,080 people every day during three months to end May 2009.

⇨ 3,300 people reported they had become redundant every day during three months to end May 2009.

⇨ The average house has decreased in value by £62 every day during the last 12 months.

⇨ £431m is the amount that the Government Public Sector net debt (PSDN) will grow today (equivalent to £5,000 per second).

⇨ £76m is the interest the Government has to pay each day on

### Striking numbers

*One in 33 people in work...*
...estimated to become unemployed in 2009.
*£58,320...*
...average household debt (including mortgages).
*£182m*
...interest paid in UK daily.
*Every ten minutes...*
...a property is repossessed.
*3,300 people...*
...made redundant every day.
*One person every 4.35 minutes...*
...declared bankrupt or insolvent.
*£5,000 a second...*
...increase in Government national debt.

the UK's net debt of £799bn. This is projected to rise to £118m a day (£43bn) in 2010-11 financial year.

⇨ 33,600 applications for credit have been turned down every day during the past six months.

⇨ 251 mortgage possession claims will be issued and 189 mortgage possession orders will be made today.

⇨ 397 landlord possession claims will be issued and 305 landlord possession orders will be made today.

⇨ 20.8m plastic card purchase transactions will be made today with a total value of £1.03bn.

⇨ Citizens Advice Bureaux dealt with 7,423 new debt problems every day.

⇨ The average car will cost £16.80 to run today.

⇨ £578m will be withdrawn from cash machines today.

*1 August 2009*

⇨ The above information is reprinted with kind permission from Credit Action. Visit www.creditaction.org.uk for more information.

© Credit Action

# Debt problems spread to the more affluent

## Information from the Consumer Credit Counselling Service

Debt problems are becoming more complex and harder to resolve as the effects of the recession begin to affect a wider cross-section of society, according to the UK's leading debt charity, Consumer Credit Counselling Service (CCCS).

In its review of client experiences over the last three years published today (March 18) in its *Statistical Yearbook 2008*, CCCS has found that although people with debt problems are better off and owe less money (with the exception of the over-60s), they are finding it harder to repay their debts.

This is likely to be because the combination of rising unemployment and a falling housing market is creating a fundamental shift in the nature of the UK's debt problem, as Malcolm Hurlston, CCCS chairman explains:

'In cases of pure overborrowing where the debtor remains in work, there continues to be an income stream to service the mortgage and, at least in part, the unsecured debts. However, when unemployment triggers a debt problem, the fall in income can leave the borrower struggling to service both mortgage and unsecured debts, while the fall in house prices, and growth in negative equity, takes away the option of selling to clear the mortgage.

'As over-indebtedness becomes a problem for the more affluent, people who come to us are more likely to have mortgages and to lead complex financial lives – homeowners owe on average 83 per cent more than renters – as a result, our task in providing best advice is bound to be more difficult and time consuming.

'Increasingly we find people need more than one counselling session before a solution can be proposed. This is particularly marked for homeowners and the self-employed. It is a trend that we expect to intensify in the coming months as the recession deepens.'

Despite the growing affluence of the CCCS client base, fewer people are in a position to repay their debts: in 2008 only about a third of clients (35 per cent) were able to commit to a Debt Management Plan (DMP) compared with 42 per cent in 2007 and 46 per cent in 2006.

Even clients able to undertake a repayment plan are finding it more difficult to maintain payments: calls to client aftercare have been steadily increasing in the last two years.

'External forces over which the credit industry has no control, including recession, unemployment, increases in the costs of everyday living and a falling housing market are compounding the problem of debt,' concludes Malcolm Hurlston. 'These trends seem likely to continue for the foreseeable future: the perfect storm may have arrived but we have yet to reach its epicentre.'

### Summary of main findings 2008

*Clients*
- ⇨ Despite falls in the amount of money owed, both in absolute terms and relative to income, fewer clients had the means to repay their debts in 2008. 35 per cent were recommended to a Debt Management Plan compared with 42 per cent in 2007 and 46 per cent in 2006 while the number of clients recommended to token payments is rising.
- ⇨ Clients seeking help are becoming more affluent: 12 per cent have net household incomes of more than £30,000 a year and nearly half (47.4 per cent) of those seeking help were homeowners. Homeowners owe on average 83 per cent more than renters.
- ⇨ Clients' problems are becoming more complicated: last year over a third required more than one counselling session before a solution could be proposed. This is particularly marked for those with mortgage arrears and the self-employed.
- ⇨ Calls to client aftercare have increased by a third in the last two years, suggesting that clients are finding it more difficult to maintain their repayment plans. This is likely to be caused by increasing pressures on household budgets.
- ⇨ The vast majority (90 per cent) of CCCS client debts are on credit cards and personal loans, the average client owes over £14,000 on each of these items.

*Regional*
- ⇨ The highest levels of debt are in the south of England but the over-60s in Wales have one of the highest debt levels in the UK at £35,947.
- ⇨ Clients in Northern Ireland, despite having significantly lower levels of borrowing are least able to repay their debts.
- ⇨ Scottish clients have the highest levels of debt in the UK relative to their income.

*Service*
- ⇨ By the close of 2008 CCCS was managing almost £3 billion worth of debt, and repaying over £224 million of this per annum.
- ⇨ The charity's helpline team received 267,000 calls in 2008, a five per cent increase on 2007 but fewer than in 2006. Only in the last quarter of 2008 did the number of helpline calls start to overtake 2006.
- ⇨ There were almost 100,000 unique users of CCCS's online debt management tool, Debt Remedy, during the year. Debt Remedy is free and anonymous.

*18 March 2009*
- ⇨ Information from the Consumer Credit Counselling Service. Visit www.cccs.co.uk for more.

# Research warns of deepening debt crisis

## Many have no hope of paying off debts in their lifetime, say Citizens Advice

New research published today points to a deepening debt crisis in which many people turning to Citizens Advice Bureaux for help have no realistic hope of paying off their debts in their lifetime.

A *life in debt* reveals that CAB debt clients owe an average of £16,971 – two thirds more than in 2001, and the equivalent of almost 18 times their total monthly household income. It will take them an average of 93 years to pay off the money they owe at a rate they can afford.

Citizens Advice Bureaux have seen debt enquiries double in the last ten years. Debt is now the number one issue advised on in bureaux, accounting for one in three of all enquiries, and CAB advisers are currently dealing with an average of 7,241* new debt problems every working day.

An in-depth analysis of data from over 1,400 debt clients found nearly one in three had mortgage or rent arrears, or owed money on secured loans. Four in ten were living in fuel poverty and a quarter had council tax arrears.

More than half had debts on at least four essential household bills and the amount owed on these was 38% higher than when similar research was last carried out in 2004.

Nearly half the homeowners (45%) had mortgage or secured loans arrears – up from 30% in 2004 – and two thirds of these would be in priority need for re-housing if they became homeless. Almost one in three (30%) spent at least half their monthly income on their mortgage and nearly one in five had no equity in their homes or were in negative equity.

One in ten had at least ten credit debts – credit cards, overdrafts, personal loans and HP – but well over half (58%) had no available income to pay these debts, a substantial increase from 2004.

The most common reasons for debt were low income, over-commitment, illness or disability and job loss. But irresponsible lending, poor financial skills and big increases in the cost of living – especially on petrol, energy, water and council tax – had also played a significant part in people's debt problems.

> **CAB debt clients owe an average of £16,971 – two thirds more than in 2001, and the equivalent of almost 18 times their total monthly household income**

CAB debt clients tend to be poorer than the population at large, with an average net monthly household income of £1,021 – less than two-thirds the national average. The average spent on housekeeping per week was £69.50, far below the national weekly average of £142.

Citizens Advice Chief Executive David Harker said:

'These findings make sobering reading, especially as they are based on data collected just before the worst of the credit crunch began to bite. Since then we have seen an enormous rise in the number of people turning to us for help because they have lost their job, so we can expect to see many more people struggling with severe debt problems as the recession continues to take its toll.

'Low income, combined with irresponsible lending, unreasonable debt collection practices and badly informed financial decisions are at the root of many of our clients' debt problems. For many there is little prospect of their income increasing or their circumstances changing. The reality is that they are condemned to a lifetime of poverty overshadowed by an inescapable burden of unpayable debt.

'In the current climate it is absolutely vital that lenders and creditors treat people fairly and sympathetically and do everything they can to help ease their debt problems and avoid adding to them. Those for whom

there seems no light at the end of the tunnel also need solutions that can offer them a fresh start, lift them out of the poverty trap, and give them a chance to build better financial skills for the future.'

Citizens Advice estimates that nearly a third of CAB debt clients could be eligible for the debt relief order** (DRO), a new alternative to bankruptcy that comes into force in April 2009. While welcoming this new debt remedy, Citizens Advice is also urging the Government to press ahead with plans to extend the range of low cost, out of court debt remedies targeted at debtors with low incomes and assets.

Cases reported recently by bureaux include:

A lone parent with three children was suffering from serious depression and had attempted suicide several times following domestic violence and a relationship breakdown. She had a number of debts including a £706 fuel bill which was being collected at £10 per week via her pre-payment meter. She could not afford her basic living expenses and was falling into debt with other household bills. At the time of seeking advice, she relied on her local church delivering food parcels.

A woman who was unable to work following an accident and was now living on benefits told the CAB that she could not afford to put the heating on this winter and was terrified of getting further into debt. She had borrowed a ski suit from a friend to wear to keep her warm in her house.

A man with £60,000 of credit debts and mortgage arrears was about to have his home repossessed. He had decided that the best way forward to clear his debts was to go bankrupt, but he could not afford the £495 court fees to petition for bankruptcy.

### Notes on the report

*A life in debt: The profile of CAB debt clients in 2008*, based on an in-depth analysis of survey data involving 1,407 new debt clients seen in 52 Citizens Advice Bureaux in England and Wales in July 2008, is available at www. citizensadvice.org.uk/a_life_in_debt or from the press office.

## Standard of living – trends

The things people can buy and do – their housing, furniture, food, cars, recreation and travel – make up their standard of living. How satisfied or dissatisfied do you feel about your standard of living at present?

* 'Neither satisfied nor dissatisfied' category for 1988 includes 'Don't know' answers.

Fieldwork: 1988-2009. Source: Ipsos MORI, April 2009.

### Key findings:

⇨ On average CAB debt clients owed £16,971 in 2008, two thirds higher than in 2001.

⇨ More than half of the clients in 2008 had four or more priority debts, such as mortgage or rent arrears, fuel bills or council tax arrears.

⇨ One client in ten had 10 credit debts or more.

⇨ 45 per cent of the home-owners had mortgage or secured loans arrears in 2008, up from 30 per cent in 2004.

⇨ 30 per cent of the homeowners spent half or more of their monthly income on housing costs.

⇨ Two thirds of the homeowners with mortgage or secured loans arrears were in priority need for rehousing.

⇨ 43 per cent of the CAB debt clients in 2008 were in fuel poverty because they spent more than ten per cent of their income on fuel.

⇨ Half of CAB debt clients were in water poverty because they spent more than three per cent of their income on water.

⇨ More than half of the clients (58 per cent) had no spare money to pay their credit debts.

⇨ Clients who had spare money to pay their debts would take on average 93 years to repay them in full.

⇨ Nearly a third of CAB clients could be eligible for the debt relief order* (DRO), a new alternative to bankruptcy which comes into force in April 2009.

### Additional notes

\* This figure is based on a daily average for the financial year to date: 1 April 2008 to 31 January 2009.

\*\* Debt relief order – is a new type of debt remedy available from April 2009 that provides an alternative to bankruptcy. It is aimed at people who are not homeowners, have less than £15,000 in debt, less than £300 in assets and less than £50 per month available income after they have met all their essential expenditure. As with bankruptcy, people will be discharged within a year and, with a few exceptions, any remaining debts will be written off. There will be a one-off flat fee of £90, with no further charges. People will have to apply for a debt relief order via an authorised intermediary. Authorised intermediaries will include CAB debt advisers.

*26 February 2009*

⇨ The above information is reprinted with kind permission from Citizens Advice. Visit www.adviceguide.org. uk for more information.

© *Citizens Advice*

# Forms of payment

## Information from Nationwide Education

You can pay for things in several ways, but which way is best?

### Cash

⇨ Cash is often the easiest if you are buying small everyday things.

⇨ Most people will take cash, and actually handing over coins and notes lets you monitor how much you're spending.

⇨ Make sure you keep receipts though, so you have a record of what you have bought and how much you've spent.

---

## You can have a credit card from the age of 18

---

⇨ If it's lost or stolen, it's gone forever, so make sure you keep it safe in a purse or wallet in a bag or deep pocket. And never send cash in the post!

### Cheque

⇨ Cheques are printed pieces of paper used instead of handling cash. Cheques draw money from your building society or bank 'current' account.

⇨ You can get a cheque book, but not until you are 16.

⇨ It's quite a safe way to pay, as it can only be 'cashed' by whoever is named on the cheque. You can therefore safely send cheques through the post.

⇨ You have to fill in the cheque stating who you are paying, how much, and then date and sign it. Often you will be asked to show a 'cheque guarantee card', which guarantees that the building society or bank will pay the money, even if you don't have enough in your account. For this to happen, you'll need to have an overdraft facility set up on your account.

⇨ But if not, when there is no money in your account and the bank won't pay the money owed, the cheque is said to 'bounce' and you are usually charged.

⇨ When you get a cheque as a gift or a payment made to you, you need to go to the bank or building society to pay the money into your account. It will take between three and five days for that money to be in your account ready for you to spend. This is an inter-bank 'clearing' process.

⇨ Some businesses don't like cheques and won't take them as payment, as they want to be paid straight away and not wait for the money to 'clear' (be in their account).

### Cash card

⇨ This is a small plastic card that can be used in ATMs (Automated Teller Machines) outside building societies, banks, supermarkets, etc, to get cash out of your account. Some building society and bank accounts let you have a cash card from the age of 12.

⇨ Each time you need to take cash out, you have to push the card in the machine and type in your special PIN (Personal Identification Number). Make sure you remember this number – it is unique to you, so never let anyone else know it!

⇨ You can only take out the money you have in the account, not borrow money.

### Debit card

⇨ A debit card is a small plastic card, used instead of cash to buy things.

⇨ You can only use it to spend the money that you actually have in your account (unless you have made a special agreement with the building society or bank).

⇨ You use it with your PIN to get money from your account at an ATM or 'cash point' and to pay for things in stores.

⇨ Make sure you remember your PIN and never give it to anyone else.

⇨ Some debit cards also act as cheque guarantee cards.

### Travellers' cheque

⇨ If you are going on holiday it's a good idea to take travellers' cheques.

⇨ These are special cheques that can be used abroad, in that country's currency. You can use

Would you accept a cheque?

TELLER

the travellers' cheques at any age but you will need your passport to get them. You sign them as soon as you get them and when you cash them, you sign again showing your ID.

⇨ They can be cashed at banks, exchange bureaux and some shops, restaurants, etc, and then used exactly like cash.

⇨ They are much safer than cash, as each cheque has a unique serial number. You keep the list of numbers separate from the cheques, and if they are lost or stolen, they can be replaced.

⇨ Be careful though – there are sometimes charges to use travellers' cheques.

### Credit card

⇨ This is a small plastic card used instead of cash to buy things. It's really a way of borrowing money as you buy something, and then pay for it later when you get your monthly credit card statement.

⇨ You can have a credit card from the age of 18.

⇨ You will be given an amount that you are allowed to spend each month. This is your 'credit limit'.

⇨ You are sent a monthly statement showing how much you spent, the total you owe and the minimum amount of money you have to pay back that month. For the amount that is left unpaid, you are charged interest.

⇨ The longer you take to pay it back, the more interest you will be charged. (It's always a good idea to pay off your credit card in full each month if you can ... but you must make sure you pay the minimum amount stated.)

⇨ You can use credit cards all over the world, and online, or over the phone.

⇨ If using a credit card in a store or restaurant you will need to use your PIN (Personal Identification Number). Make sure you don't let others know or see this number or they could use your card to get money or goods.

Credit cards do have disadvantages though:

⇨ There are often charges, e.g. for late payment or use abroad.

⇨ It can be easy to lose track of what you are spending.

⇨ The card, or your details, can be stolen. Always check your monthly statement!

### Store card

⇨ A store card is a special credit card which you can use to buy things in that store only, again using borrowed money.

⇨ You get a monthly statement like other credit cards and a minimum payment must be made. If you don't pay the total amount, you pay interest.

⇨ Be careful though, they often have a much higher rate of interest than a credit card and don't allow you to borrow as much money!

There are other ways of making a payment:

### Direct debit

⇨ Direct debit payments are agreed with your building society or bank to pay regular bills from your account.

⇨ The amount paid out may differ from bill to bill. It is determined by the recipient (the person receiving money) and you should be informed of the amount (e.g. you set up a direct debit to pay your mobile phone bill every month, but you don't know in advance how much you will use your phone each month. Your phone company tells your building society or bank exactly how much you owe for that month and the money is then transferred to them electronically).

⇨ Direct debits make paying very easy but you still need to take care and check your statements every month – companies sometimes make mistakes! You must always check that you have enough money in your account to cover the bill; otherwise the bank may not pay and you may be charged a penalty.

### Standing order

⇨ Standing orders are another sort of agreement with your building

society or bank to make regular payments, but these are for an exact amount of money each month. You determine the amount.

⇨ It is similar to a direct debit but the amount paid every month is the same. It might be used to pay the rent or digital television bills or transfer regular amounts of money to a savings account.

### Electronic transfer and Internet banking

⇨ Internet banking is when you bank online through your computer instead of going to the actual building society or bank.

⇨ Payments are easy and instant, as money is transferred from your bank account to someone else's.

⇨ This can be organised either online or by phone. However, there are security issues!

TIP – Never give out your bank details unless you are certain about the organisation you are paying. Never respond to emails asking for your PIN and bank details, no matter who they appear to be from.

⇨ The above information is taken from the *Financial Capability – Forms of Payment* fact sheet produced by Nationwide Education and is reproduced with permission. Visit www.Nationwide Education.co.uk for more information.

*© Nationwide Education*

# Boosting credit card limits

## Credit card providers throw £8.8billion of unrequested credit at consumers

⇨ In just 12 months, 5.7 million people have received a boost to their credit card limit without their consent whilst 3% have seen their spending power slashed.

⇨ The average increase received was £1,538, bolstering these limits from £5,129 to £6,667 and increasing the average interest bill from £800 to £1,040.

⇨ These consumers have a total of £8.8 billion additional cash to splash and could face an annual interest bill of £5.9 billion.

⇨ Across the board, over 9.3 million (31%) consumers have had their credit card limit increased or decreased in the last 12 months.

⇨ More than one in ten (four million) people found themselves short of cash and actually applied for an increase – 31% of these were turned down.

As the Government's spotlight shines on the UK's credit card market in today's white paper, new research from uSwitch. com reveals that 5.7 million consumers have seen their credit limit increased by an average of £1,538 in the past 12 months without their consent. In total, these consumers have received an additional £8.8 billion of credit. If these consumers max out their new credit limit, they could now face an annual interest bill of £1040 each or £5.9 billion in total. 3% of people received an even bigger shock when their credit limit was slashed without their permission.

In total, 31% of all credit card customers have seen their credit card limit move in one direction or another over the past 12 months, 90% of these have been increased by a staggering £13 billion. With the average credit card limit at £5,129, this now gives them a total of £6,667 to spend. In total, almost four million consumers (13%) actually approached their provider to request an increase to their credit limit and just under a third of these (4%) were rejected.

Louise Bond, personal finance expert at uSwitch.com, comments: 'In the current climate you could be fooled into thinking that increasing credit limits without permission is a good thing as it stops people going over their limits and incurring extra charges. However, the issue is far more complicated as providers are taking away consumer choice by throwing extra credit at people without their consent. There is also a question mark around how these people are selected for an increase or decrease to their limit and if this in itself is in the customer's best interest.

'Unless you are one of the 68% of consumers that regularly pay their credit card bill in full, keeping high levels of debt on interest-bearing credit cards isn't advisable as it's an expensive form of borrowing. In most cases, providers really aren't helping consumers by throwing cash at them as it could be placing unnecessary temptation in their path.'

Credit cards are still an expensive way to borrow money if they aren't used correctly. Fees and charges on these cards are constantly climbing with purchases APRs jumping up by 0.74% in the last year alone from 16.95% to 17.69%. For larger debts that cannot be paid off over a shorter period of time an unsecured personal loan really is a cheaper option with average APRs currently at 9.07% – 8.62% lower than the average credit card rate.
*2 July 2009*

⇨ The above information is reprinted with kind permission from uSwitch. Visit www.uswitch.com for more information.

*© uSwitch*

# Cashless society favoured by four in ten shoppers

## Information from Talking Retail

Four out of ten consumers say they would rather pay for all transactions by card, according to research by payment solutions company RBS WorldPay.

But half of retailers think there is nothing they can do to improve payment systems, the study found.

Half (52%) of retailers surveyed said upgrading their card payment solutions had a positive impact on their business, increasing profits by an average 18%. One in four claimed profitability increased between 25% and 50%.

But one in five said they do not undertake any research to find the right payment system for their business and half do not think there is anything they could do to improve the payment technology they offer consumers.

However, seven out of ten customers said they wanted faster, less hassle and more secure payment solutions. 67% of consumers wished independent retail outlets offered more card solutions and nearly half of consumers said they would rather pay for all transactions by card.

- 42% said their lives would be much easier if they could pay for everything with cards rather than cash.
- 49% expect the UK to become a near cashless society by 2030 and 39% expect to only use one piece of technology for all payment transactions.
- 29% expect to soon pay for goods and services with automated face recognition.
- 35% of consumers expect to soon pay for goods and services with iris recognition.
- 24% believe that one day micro-dots will be inserted into our hands to enable people to truly 'wave and pay'.
- 54% of retailers said customers still regularly pay for goods by cheque.

Some 52% of retailers believe there will be a cashless society, but seven in ten said they would not be in a position to accept contactless cards within the next five years.

Fewer than one in ten (8%) of general retailers currently has the technology to accept contactless card payments, despite six in ten (63%) thinking that within ten years most people will buy most small value products with the wave of a card or handheld device.

Six in ten (59%) of consumers said they were too embarrassed to pay for small items with cards.
*23 April 2009*

- The above information is reprinted with kind permission from Talking Retail. Visit www.talkingretail.com for more information.

© *Talking Retail*

# Report states that cash is still king, but for how long?

## Information from UK Payments Administration Limited

*2008 cash and cash machine data shows:*
- *71% of all cash acquired by consumers came from cash machines. 2.9 billion cash machine withdrawals were made last year – equivalent to 91 withdrawals per second;*
- *Cash payment volumes are forecast to fall by 27% over the next 10 years;*
- *If current trends persist, next year for the first time debit card spending will overtake cash spending by value.*

The payment industry's latest publication, *The Way We Pay 2009: UK Cash & Cash Machines* provides the latest data on how UK consumers are obtaining and using cash and how this is forecast to change. The full Payments Council report issued this month (June 2009) includes data from Link and other industry sources.

Whilst cash spending continues to remain relatively flat, the number of cash machine withdrawals continues to rise and is forecast to peak in 2011. Consumers are increasingly using cash machines for withdrawing cash, where previously they would have withdrawn money in bank branches or at post offices; five years ago only 54% of cash came from cash machines, last year 71% of cash was acquired that way. This shift has been driven by an increase in the availability and numbers of cash machines as well as the migration of payment for state benefits and pensions to automated methods.

The report also reveals that in 2008, consumers made 22.4 billion cash payments, amounting to a total value of £267 billion, and that UK cash machines paid out £192 billion in 2.9 billion transactions. By contrast, in 2008, debit cardholders made 5.5 billion purchases and spent £247 billion on their cards. Although consumer cash spending still amounts to more than that by any other single payment method, this may not remain the case for long – in 2010 consumer debit card spending is forecast to outstrip cash spending by value for the first time.*

Edwin Latter, scheme director of Link, said:

'The report provides a clear picture of the nation's usage and acquisition of cash, revealing how often we withdraw cash as well as the types of places where we make cash payments and what we buy there. For example, two-thirds of cash payments, by volume, last year were made in shops, and 5% of all the cash payments spent there were on entries to the National Lottery.

'Even though the report predicts that cash transactions by value could be overtaken by debits cards for the

first time next year, no-one is claiming that the end of cash is nigh. By volume cash still remains king, and will remain so until a viable alternative for low value transactions is widely available.'

*On 29 December 2004 total spending on debit, credit and charge cards exceeded cash for the first time (£269 billion against £268 billion)*

Some additional facts and figures from *The Way We Pay 2009: UK Cash & Cash Machines*:

⇨ In 1998, 80% of payments were made by cash, as opposed to 66% last year.

⇨ Of the total 22.4 billion cash payments made last year, 13.9 billion were for payments of £5 or less.

⇨ In 2008, 98% of adults were cash users.

⇨ In the UK, by the end of 2008 there were 63,916 cash machines, 97% of cash withdrawn was from free-to-use cash machines.

⇨ In 2008 there was a small increase in the per machine average amounts of cash withdrawn from bank and building society machines, whereas the average amounts of cash withdrawn at independent cash machines fell by 3.2% last year.

⇨ In 2008, cash machines paid out £192 billion – equivalent to £6,094 per second.

⇨ The use of debit card cashback remains limited and, in fact, has fallen for the last three years, with

£6.7 billion paid out in cashback last year as opposed to £7.2 billion in 2005.

⇨ 9,750 mini-statements were printed at each cash machine offering the service last year.

⇨ In 2007, the Irish and British made the most cash machine withdrawals per head when compared with other EU nationalities.

*3 June 2009*

⇨ The above information is reprinted with permission from UK Payments Administration Ltd. UK Payments Administration Ltd can accept no liability that may arise from any third party's reliance on this material.

*© UK Payments Administration Ltd*

# Women and financial independence

## Global survey shows six in ten women consider themselves financially independent

Leading global market intelligence firm Synovate today released results from a new study on women and financial independence, which found that nearly six in ten (58%) women across 12 diverse countries believe themselves to be financially independent.

### Most emphatically independent were French women with 80% considering themselves financially autonomous, followed by British women (76%) and South African women (69%)

Most emphatically independent were French women with 80% considering themselves financially autonomous, followed by British women (76%) and South African women (69%).

The survey looked at the roles women around the world play in their household finances; whether they feel in control of their own cash; how many women believe they are financially independent; as well as attitudes on whether women are better with money than men. Synovate spoke with around 4,500 women and also posed some questions to the same number of men.

### Why women?

Synovate's Senior Vice President of Financial Services in the US, Claire Braverman, explained why Synovate took a particular interest in women and finances in this survey.

'A woman meets a man, falls in love, moves in, gets married, has kids (not necessarily in that order) and it all falls apart. It's not until this moment that she realises just how dependent she is on her partner's money.

'Some women have checks in place to guard against this happening to them; some don't. Some are financially savvy, and some are simply not interested.

'And even if a relationship break up is not a catalyst, women live longer than men and typically have less money upon retirement.

'All this adds up to an urgent need for financial services companies to understand women and cater to their specific needs and the situations in which they are likely to find themselves, planned or unplanned,' she said.

### Sisters doing it for themselves

Braverman continued: 'It's not many decades since women started entering the workforce *en masse* and, to varying degrees, some aspects of gender equality remain unaddressed in every country of the world. Yet the survey found that nearly six in ten women across 12 diverse countries believe themselves to be financially independent. That's certainly encouraging,' she said.

Least likely to consider themselves financially independent were women in Bulgaria (where 37% said they were independent) and Indonesia (47%). Overall, the developed economies surveyed were significantly more likely to have women who consider themselves financially independent than the emerging economies (68% versus 51%).

Braverman says that American women were particularly intriguing in terms of their perceived financial independence.

'While 64% of American women feel financially independent, that leaves more than a third of us who do not. For a nation that prides itself on an independent spirit, this is surprising.

'It may be that American women have higher expectations of what financial independence actually means. In part, there are a lot of women in marriages and partnerships who willingly cede monetary control, and there are an alarming number of women (often single mothers) in risky financial situations.'

Also fascinating is the South African situation. The relatively new democracy is one of the six still-developing economies surveyed but is apparently filled with self-sufficient women. Seven in ten women said they were financially independent, even more than in the majority of the developed markets that were surveyed.

Synovate South Africa's Client Services Director for Financial Services, Debbie Amm, said: 'This is partly because the women we spoke with were largely urban, but there are greater cultural and historical explanations at hand too.

'Since South Africa became a democracy there has been a very strong and very public focus on gender equality, providing opportunities for women to advance careers or simply to start one.

'Equally, in both black and white histories, there has always been a need for women to be able to look after themselves and their families. South Africa can be a tough place, so this need for self-sufficiency has given rise to a highly entrepreneurial mindset among the women of the nation,' she said.

### Breadwinning broads or ladies who lunch?

The survey also asked women to choose what the term 'financial independence' meant to them. The top three answers across all 12 markets surveyed were 'Financial independence is about not being dependent on my husband or partner for money' (41%), 'Financial independence is about living debt free' (30%) and 'Financial independence is about being able to afford the things I want without worrying about the cost' (18%).

The feisty French were most likely to equate financial independence with not having to rely on a partner for money (68%), followed by Dutch and British women (both 51%).

Doing without debt is key for 42% of Malaysian and 40% of Mexican women who chose this as their top definition of financial independence.

A standout 42% of Bulgarian women think financial independence means being able to afford what they want without worrying about the cost. This is more than double the number who chose that definition in most other markets (other than Malaysia, which had the second-highest response at 22%).

Stoyan Mihaylov, Synovate Bulgaria's Managing Director, explains why: 'It may surprise some from other parts of the world, but the prevailing family model in Bulgaria is for both partners to be equal bread winners. At the same time, women are responsible for running the household.

'There are two main reasons for this. First, during the socialist period both genders were practically equalised by income. After that time the differentiation of incomes in favour of men took place, although a decline in living standards pushed women into working and therefore preserved the model. Throughout all this, women remained the housekeepers.

'Thus women's spending is restricted by the dual responsibilities they have. The dream of independence is not one of freedom from a husband-as-provider but one of having the freedom to personally provide for the wellbeing of the family, able to afford needs and wants regardless of the cost,' he said.

### Man the head of the house?

The survey also explored men's and women's attitudes about male roles in household finance, finding that an overall 43% of women agreed that 'a man should be responsible for the mortgage/house payments'. When the same question was posed to male respondents, 53% agreed, showing men are more likely to consider themselves more responsible for this part of the household budget.

Naturally, there is a great deal of discrepancy in the findings across markets. Standouts are:

⇨ Indonesia where 83% of men and 82% of women agree that 'a man should be responsible for the mortgage/house payments';

⇨ The Netherlands where only 15% of men and 7% of women agree with this statement;

⇨ The UK where 48% of men versus 15% of women agree;

⇨ Similarly, France where 47% of men believe they are responsible but only 18% of women agree;

⇨ Australia with 34% of men and only 12% of women agreeing.

The survey also asked whether providing for the family is a man's responsibility. Overall, 58% of men and 38% of women agreed. The two Asian countries surveyed were most likely to agree, with an overall 87% in Indonesia and 73% in Malaysia putting the onus on men.

Managing Director of Synovate in Malaysia, Steve Murphy, said: 'This shows the traditional nature of Malaysia where the man is still very much seen as the main breadwinner for the family. The role of the male is established very early, firmly and consistently.

'Of course this does not mean that women have nothing to do with the money. In many cases, Malaysian women control the purse strings,' he said.

Similarly, when asked whether 'a man should be responsible for looking after the financial needs of his wife or partner', the more traditional cultures were most in favour. Overall, 51% agreed, made up of 57% men and 45% women.

A near-universal 95% of both genders agreed in Indonesia and Robby Susatyo, Synovate's Managing Director for Indonesia, explains why.

'This is 100% cultural. For centuries, women did not engage in paid work or earn a living. Until quite recently, when urban Indonesians began widespread use of banking systems, husbands would surrender all their income to their wives for them to manage.

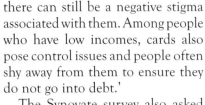

'Today, women's participation in the labour force in big cities is about 37% but the mindset remains. She does it to supplement the household income and her husband does the monetary "heavy lifting". In Islamic law, the husband is obliged to disclose all his personal wealth to his wife, but not the other way around,' he said.

## Miss Responsible meets Lady Luck

Just over half of all respondents (both men and women) agreed that 'women are more responsible with money than men'. Perhaps not surprisingly there is a significant difference across gender – 61% of women think the fairer sex is more responsible with money but only 40% of men agree.

The highest level of agreement was found in Mexico with an overall 72%, comprised of 82% women and 62% men.

Evelyn Jabiles, Managing Director of Synovate in Mexico, was not overly surprised. 'Mexican women commonly play the role of home administrators, handing out money for utilities, rent, credit cards, school and medical fees and so on. They know what's coming in, and what's going out.

'Women here tend to think of men as "big spenders" and somewhat irresponsible,' Jabiles said.

It appears many women like to be in control of the household money, but some take their chances as well. 13% of women across the markets surveyed buy lottery tickets or enter raffles and competitions in an effort to become financially independent or maintain that status.

Women who wager were most likely to be found in Australia where 35% 'have a go', or the UK where 31% join them.

Synovate Australia's Managing Director, Julie Beeck, says: 'The Australian market for lottery products is mature, with a high incidence of participation. The dream of winning big and changing your life overnight is very much alive, and even more so in such uncertain economic times.'

## Credit where it's due

How people feel about credit tends to evolve as credit card use matures in a country. Overall, 42% of our female respondents use part of their monthly income towards credit card payments.

The highest credit card use was in Canada at 77%, France at 72% and the US and Australia, both at 71%. The lowest use was 2% in Indonesia, 12% in Bulgaria and 19% in Malaysia.

Claire Braverman says that credit cards have had a negative image from the beginning, but convenience and rewards can make them a very attractive proposition.

'Some decades ago, when credit cards were first introduced, there was a dislike for debt and cash was king. Relying on credit meant you could not afford what you were buying.

'As people started using cards, that image switched to one of convenience. So in countries where the cards have become entrenched, they have been embraced for their ease of use and loyalty programmes.

'In countries where the use of credit cards is relatively new,

there can still be a negative stigma associated with them. Among people who have low incomes, cards also pose control issues and people often shy away from them to ensure they do not go into debt.'

The Synovate survey also asked people whether they agreed with the statement: 'Having more than one credit card can lead to financial debt.' Overall 70% of women agreed, led by 90% of Mexican women.

Braverman continues: 'It's obviously not the card itself that causes anyone to use it. So the statement is really about control and temptation. The ability to spend more, money that you don't have in the first place, can certainly lead to debt. It means people have to control themselves and their spouses. Not always easy!'

Evelyn Jabiles explains the danger in Mexico: 'In Mexico, credit cards are perceived as "extra money" rather than a line of credit, which is why they are considered dangerous by many. Interest rates on the cards are extremely high, which only adds to the risk of debt.'

## Curiosities

⇨ 47% of women believe that women spend more money than men – and 56% of men agree with them. Chances are high that much of this 'big spending' is done on behalf of the family.

⇨ Brazilian and South African women are the most proactive when it comes to taking actions to become financially independent or stay that way. An example? 83% of Brazilian women and 71% of South African women make their own financial plans and/or budgets.

⇨ 80% of people believe it's important to know about financial products and services offered by banks and insurance companies, led by South Africa (95%), the US (91%) and Canada (91%).

2 March 2009

⇨ The above information is reprinted with kind permission from Synovate. Visit www.synovate.com for more information on this and other related topics.

# What age can I work?

### Information from CLIC

⇨ You might find that the pocket money you get from your parents or guardians is not quite enough for some of the things you would like to do or buy, especially as you get older and may be your parents or guardian are not able to afford to give you more. Also they may think it is a good idea that you find out how long it takes to earn say £5 and that to spend it quickly on a CD is not always a good thing.

⇨ If you are trying to save up for something special or find you need more money to do the things you want to do, you could think about getting a part-time job.

⇨ Generally, you can get a full or part-time job of your choice once you are 16 years old.

⇨ No-one under the age of 16 can be employed in work, other than 'light work'. Check with your local authority about what work you can do. Some local authorities also have extra rules about children working under the age of 16. These are called by-laws. Please check with your local authority for information on the by-laws in your area.

⇨ If you are under 14, you are not allowed to work at all, except in the following circumstances:
  ↳ To take part in sport, advertising, modelling, plays, films, TV or other entertainment, although your employer would need a license first;
  ↳ To do odd jobs for parents, relatives or neighbours

---

## No-one under the age of 16 can be employed in work, other than 'light work'

---

  ↳ To do baby-sitting. There is no age restriction on working as a baby-sitter;
  ↳ There are strict rules about working under the age of 18, so know your rights before you start working. Find out about working hours, working conditions, wages and your rights by visiting the Law Rights and Citizenship or Employment sections of the CLIC website or by talking to your local Citizens Advice Bureau (details below).

⇨ If you are under 16 and working, you do not pay national insurance on your wages and will not have to pay income tax unless you earn over £4,195 a year.

⇨ If you do decide to get a job to earn some extra money, make sure it does not interfere with your education. A part-time job might give you a few more pounds in your pocket now, but it is no substitute for a good education and a future career.

### For more information and advice, visit the links below:
*Money Stuff*
Advice on pocket money for 11-16 year olds.
http://www.parentspenniespounds.co.uk/kids/pocket_money_1416.html
*Citizens Advice Bureau*
Advice on young people and employment in Wales.
http://www.adviceguide.org.uk/wales/life/employment/young_people_and_employment.htm
*Need 2 Know*
A comprehensive guide to money and finances for young people.
http://www.need2know.co.uk/money/savings/article.html/id=416
*Childline*
Free and confidential helpline for young people.
0800 11 11
http://www.childline.org.uk

⇨ The above text was extracted with permission from CLIC, the National Information and Advice Service for young people aged 11-25 in Wales, funded by the Welsh Assembly Government. www.cliconline.co.uk

© CLIC

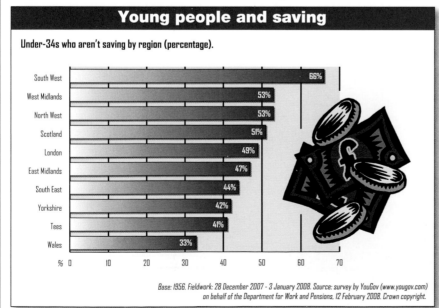

## Young people and saving

Under-34s who aren't saving by region (percentage).

| Region | Percentage |
|---|---|
| South West | 66% |
| West Midlands | 53% |
| North West | 53% |
| Scotland | 51% |
| London | 49% |
| East Midlands | 47% |
| South East | 44% |
| Yorkshire | 42% |
| Tees | 41% |
| Wales | 33% |

Base: 1956. Fieldwork: 28 December 2007 - 3 January 2008. Source: survey by YouGov (www.yougov.com) on behalf of the Department for Work and Pensions, 12 February 2008. Crown copyright.

# Younger generation look to brighter financial futures

## Information from RBS Group

NatWest unveils Year 2 findings from the MoneySense Panel – an unprecedented five-year survey of over 9,000 young people, aged 12-19 years, examining the effectiveness of financial education. It looks at earnings, budgeting, debt, and hopes and aspirations for their future finances.

The results from this year's NatWest MoneySense Panel reveal a generation becoming increasingly aware of the challenging economic times they live in, and preparing for their financial futures in ways their parents never did. With more importance placed on the personal finance curriculum in schools, there is evidence of a more financially capable generation.

- ⇨ An impressive 86% of young people keep track of their money, up from 79% last year.
- ⇨ 82% reported learning about money at home or at school last year with 77% looking up to their parents for advice on money.
- ⇨ Over two-thirds (68%) said they knew more about managing money than last year.

### Financial 'expectation gap' narrowing

Young people were asked about their financial aspirations for the future: on buying a home, a car, what they hope to earn, and then these were measured against the reality, giving us the 'expectation gap'. Although respondents still have high financial hopes for their futures, this year's findings reveal that this gap is narrowing. Last year, our economic analysis shows that in total, this expectation gap equated to at least £76,967 per person or £538,765 billion across Great Britain, which now stands at £72,133, a drop of 6% or £4,834 since last year. (£504,930 billion).

- ⇨ SALARIES: On average, young people expect to be earning an annual salary at age 35 of £53,900 (significantly more realistic than last year's £69,500). The current annual salary of adults is £23,893 at the age of 35.
- ⇨ CARS: 72% of 12-19 year olds expect to own their own car by the age of 21. Last year only one in eight drivers were aged 21.
- ⇨ DEBT: A more realistic 39% of young people believe that they will owe less than £10,000 in debt when they finish university, down from 43% last year. The actual figure is about £12,700.

### 'Home owning, debt-free, high earners' of the future

These findings paint a picture of a generation which although becoming increasingly aware of the economic climate, have optimistic expectations for their future finances. This generation predict high salaries and low debt in their financial futures; however, this expectation gap has narrowed over the past year, suggesting a more clued-up, 'realistic' future generation. While this demonstrates a more cautious approach, the good news is that they have not given up on long-term ambitions of home ownership. 58% of this generation hope to own a house by the age of 25. This translates to an estimated 2.3 million future homeowners.

### Positive and on track for brighter financial futures

With much more importance placed on financial education in schools, and more exposure to talk of money around them, it is encouraging to note some positive trends that have emerged over the past year when it comes to attitudes towards their financial situations, keeping track of their money and seeking advice on money matters. 86% of 12-19 year olds keep track of their money and 77% of them think their parents are 'good at managing money'. But in stark contrast 91% of adults have never received any form of financial education.

With young people saying they receive on average £1,500 a year (£124 per month) in the form of pocket money, monetary gifts and mobile top up credit, this is a generation clearly at ease with receiving, managing and spending money. Although only 27% are earning from household chores, in the older groups the sense of having to supplement the money they get at home is demonstrated by the number of youngsters who have part-time jobs. Nearly a quarter of 15 year olds are balancing school work with a part-time job, rising to over a third (34%) of 16 years olds and 42% of 17 year olds.

- ⇨ Half of young people are content that they 'have enough money', up from 46% last year.
- ⇨ The number of young people keeping track of their money increased by 7% from 79% last year to an impressive 86% this year. A majority (62%) expressed that they would not spend their money on things if they think they might need the money for something else. This suggests a level of planning when it comes to spending.
- ⇨ When asked how much more money per month would make them happy, this year young people came across less needy than last year citing £372 compared to £496 (25% less needy this year).

⇨ There is more acceptance of debt as a reality in life (30% up from 26% last year).

⇨ It is also encouraging that almost a quarter (23%) would consider the interest rate when thinking about borrowing money, up from only 17% last year.

### 'Hopeful Generation' coming down to earth

Salary expectations at the age of 35 stands at £53,900 – significantly lower than last year's £69,500. This compares to the current average annual earnings of only £23,893 for 30-39 year olds in Great Britain. Furthermore, the research seems to demonstrate that a young person's earning aspirations are to some extent determined by their own parents' salaries. This contrast was starkly highlighted in the findings; young people from higher earning families optimistically expect to be earning an average of £56,900 at the age of 35. This contrasts with young people from lower socio-economic groups, who estimate £12,000 less at that age – £44,200 on average.

Maxine Norris, Head of NatWest MoneySense for Schools, comments: 'The MoneySense Panel results are encouraging in that young people's attitudes and behaviours towards money seem to be moving in the right direction. This will be the first time these young people live through an economic downturn which, although challenging for their parents, may encourage greater realism when it comes to their future financial expectations. Last year the NatWest MoneySense for Schools programme delivered almost a million lessons on managing money in 60% of UK secondary schools, and we are committed to continuing this work equipping the next generation with the skills and knowledge they need to face the financial challenges ahead of them.

'Ultimately, the more exposed young people are to financial issues and the younger they become aware of them, particularly during the challenging economic climate, the more likely they are to become responsible, forward-planning adults who manage their finances confidently and effectively.'

Dr Sandra Scott, Psychological Expert, who has tracked the NatWest MoneySense Panel from the start, says: 'Young people can be remarkably influenced by changes in their parents' attitudes towards money. We may see that this change in outlook during the economic downturn could result in more savvy, informed young people with a greater understanding of how they can best shape their financial futures. The NatWest MoneySense Panel could be key in tracking the progress the next generation makes and we as parents and guardians should remember the importance of engaging our children on money matters as they develop into financially aware young adults.'

### Other key findings from the research

The panel findings revealed some dramatic differences across the country in young people's attitudes towards their future finances:

⇨ Young people in the South West are best at budgeting with 89% keeping track of their money compared to 83% in the North East, North West and Scotland.

⇨ Young people in Scotland are the most happy with the money they receive, with 59% agreeing that they always have enough money, while in the South West only 40% are content with their current financial situation.

⇨ In terms of earnings it seems young people in the North West receive a massive £140 per month compared with young people in the West Midlands who receive £84 a month on average.

⇨ 37% of young people in the SW earn money from chores while only 21% in the North West and the North East help out at home for their pocket money.

⇨ Young people in the West Midlands seem to have wised up the most when it comes to saying they would considering the interest rate when borrowing money (28%), compared to only 9% last year.

⇨ Young people in the East Midlands reported knowing more about money over the past year (75%), the highest of all the regions.

⇨ Perhaps unsurprisingly, Londoners predicted the highest salaries by the time they reach 35 – a staggering £77,400 – while those in the South West were the most realistic, predicting £33,700 (£43,700 less than Londoners).

⇨ Scottish parents seem to be the most highly regarded by their children as good at managing money – 83% reported this, compared to only 69% in the North East.

*30 March 2009*

⇨ The above information summarises the MoneySense Research Panel findings and is reprinted with kind permission from the RBS Group. Visit www.moneysensepanel.co.uk for more information.

*© RBS Group*

# Aviva identifies 'the forever generation'

## Today's youngsters could be trapped into a 'work to live' cycle into their twilight years

Today's children could become what Aviva has dubbed 'the forever generation'. They are the generation who will be retiring later, paying their mortgage for longer and having children live with them well into their twilight years

Lifestyle changes mean that people are now taking up to seven years longer to reach various milestones – leaving home, marrying, buying a house and starting a family – than they did 30 years ago. Aviva is therefore warning that people need to start planning for their retirement sooner rather than later.

### Forever mortgages

The average first-time buyer is 34 years old. If current trends continue, by 2039 the average first-time buyer would be 41 years old. With an increasing number of providers currently offering 40 year mortgages,[1] paying off a mortgage at 80 years of age could become a common phenomenon.

### Later retirement

The average age of retirement is steadily creeping upwards. Although average retirement is just over 64 years for men and nearly 62 years for women,[2] changes in state pension allowance will mean that by 2046 state pension age will rise to 68 for both men and women, forcing people to work for longer before they are able to draw a state pension.

Offspring staying at home – With the average age of a first-time buyer increasing, there is a steady increase in the number of offspring choosing to live at home later in life. More than a quarter (29%) of young men (aged 20-34) are living with their parents, a figure that has grown by 300,000 people since 2001.[3]

Darren Dicks, head of annuity propositions for Aviva UK Life, said: 'There is a risk that without forward planning, today's young adults could end up in a work-to-live cycle for what feels like "forever". Without suitable pension provision and a means to pay off their mortgage before retirement, people could find themselves having to work for much longer than they do now.

'And if people have children in their 40s who then live with them into their 30s – a trend which is currently growing[3] – people could be supporting their "children" well into what has traditionally been a time to retire and relax.

'On a more positive note, life expectancy is also increasing steadily, rising from 82.8 and 86.8 respectively for men and women born 30 years ago, to 88.5 and 91.8 for people born now.[4] So even though people are working longer, they are also living longer in retirement. This underlines the importance of planning ahead and preparing for a long life.'

Aviva has also unearthed the following 'forever generation' statistics:

⇨ The number of women having children over the age of 40 has increased by more than four times in the last 30 years, from 6,000 per year to 25,400 now.[4]

⇨ Babies born in 2039 are predicted to have a life expectancy of 92.3 years (males) and 95.1 (females).[5]

## Notes

1. Source: MoneyExpert.com
2. Source ONS, April-June 2008. Statistics refer to men and women who had worked past 50. In 1984 the average retirement age was 63.7 for men and 60.7 for women.
3. Figures published in the annual ONS 'state of the nation' report *Social Trends* show that, in the second quarter of 2008, 29% of 20- to 34-year-old men and 18% of women of the same age lived with their parents. This equated to around 1.8 million men and 1.1 million women.
4. Source: ONS: *Population Trends*: Spring 2009.
5. Source: Government Actuary's Department: Cohort Expectations of Life.
6. Source: ONS: *Population Trends*: Spring 2009. Figures compare most up-to-date information with closest comparable data from 30 years preceding.
7. Source: GE Money Home Lending.

*8 June 2009*

⇨ The above information is reprinted with kind permission from Aviva. Visit www.aviva.com for more information.

© *Aviva*

### Changing ages of milestone events

| Event | Average age 30 years ago | Average age now | Shift compared to 30 years ago | Expected age in 30 years' time |
|---|---|---|---|---|
| First marriage (men)[1] | 25.1 years | 31.9 years | 6.8 years | 38.7 years |
| First marriage (women)[1] | 22.8 years | 29.8 years | 7 years | 36.8 years |
| Birth of first child (women)[1] | 26.6 years | 29.3 years | 2.7 years | 32 years |
| Purchase of first home[2] | 27 years | 34 years | 7 years | 41 years |

1. Source: ONS: Population Trends Spring 2009. Figures compare most up-to-date information with closest comparable data from 30 years preceding.
2. Source: GE Money Home Lending.

Source: Aviva, 8 June 2009.

# The Budget 2009

**The Chancellor has just announced a new Budget. What does it mean for you?**

### What is the Budget?

The Budget is a statement made every year by the Government on where the money needed to spend on the country will come from, and what the money will be spent on.

It's worked out by the Chancellor of the Exchequer with help from his office, the Treasury. The Chancellor decides how to spend money on services like schools, hospitals, the police, housing and even youth centres and facilities.

The current Chancellor is Alistair Darling.

### Where does the money come from?

Money for the country's Budget comes from tax, including income tax, VAT and duties.

Income tax is paid by everyone who earns money in the UK – richer people have to pay more.

VAT is the tax added to some of the things we buy – 15 per cent of the cost of what we buy goes to the Government.

Duties are extra sums charged on products such as cigarettes, alcohol and petrol.

### How will it help you?

One of the main focuses for this year's Budget is helping young people secure school and college places as well as jobs when they leave. The Chancellor is also keen to help students in credit crunch times.

*18-24 year olds*

Those aged between 18-24 who have been unemployed for more than 12 months will benefit from assistance that will guarantee employment – JobCentre Plus will receive more funding so that they have more staff and resources to help people find jobs.

100,000 new jobs will be funded through local authorities and the voluntary sector. This means 18-24 year olds will have the opportunity to work in jobs that offer a lot of value to society.

BUDGET CAKE

SCHOOLS · POLICE · HOUSING · AGED CARE · ARMED SERVICES · HOSPITALS · JOB CENTRE PLUS ... CARE FIRST

The Budget has also set aside funds for new training courses and community work placements.

### Want a job in the care sector?

CareFirst, a funding scheme for providers to train and employ young people, has been introduced. This is because there are many jobs in the care sector. In fact there were 100,000 job vacancies in social care last year. Providers will get money to train and employ young people between 18 and 24 years old who have been out of work for more than 12 months.

*16-17 year olds*

The Chancellor has promised that every 16 and 17 year old that wants a place on a course will be guaranteed one in the next academic year. This promise will be met with an extra 54,500 education and training places. From this September schools and sixth forms will also receive an extra £250m to fund places for students.

The Chancellor also pledged an extra £400m for schools and colleges to pay for places for 16 and 17 year olds in the academic year 2010/11 when there is likely to be more demand for places.

That's because more students are likely to want to stay on as there might be fewer jobs. More school and sixth-form places means there are likely to be less young people who are unemployed in the long run as students will be better qualified when they leave education.

### Fast fun facts

⇨ On Budget day the Chancellor makes a speech in the Houses of Parliament to MPs.

⇨ The longest speech was made by William Gladstone on 18 April 1853, lasting four hours and forty-five minutes!

⇨ The red briefcase that you see on telly is where the Chancellor traditionally keeps his Budget speech.

⇨ The original red briefcase was first used by politician William Gladstone in 1860.

⇨ But in 1997, the then Chancellor, Gordon Brown, had a new one made – about time too!

*24 April 2009*

⇨ The above information is re-printed with kind permission from need2know. Visit www.need2know.co.uk for more information.

# Banks and building societies

## Information from the Citizenship Foundation and Abbey

### Opening an account

Although there is no minimum legal age for someone to have a bank account, most banks offer basic accounts to young people aged 11 and over. These provide a cash card, which you can use at a bank machine to withdraw cash, and possibly a debit card that will only work if there's enough money in your account. A regular current account is normally available only if you are 18 or over, or 16 or 17 with a steady income, or, an adult to act as guarantor.

### Why have an account?

⇨ many employers will only pay wages into an account;

⇨ an account is needed for a student loan;

⇨ the money can earn interest;

⇨ regular accounts come with a cheque book and card to pay for things;

⇨ you can pay cheques other people give you into an account.

### Choosing a bank or building society

Always read the small print. You will probably want to know:

⇨ whether it has a branch near you and offers online banking;

⇨ whether there are convenient cash points;

⇨ about services offered and charges;

⇨ what interest is paid on the money in your account. There will be leaflets on this, or you can ask a member of staff; and

⇨ about special offers for young people.

Don't be persuaded by offers or gifts if the services and charges are not as good as other banks or building societies.

There are two main types of accounts – current accounts and savings accounts.

### Current accounts

A current account is for day-to-day transactions. You pay in money, such as your wages or student loan, which you can draw out as you please. If you are 18 or over, you usually get a

### Words they use

**Overdraft** – An overdraft allows you to spend more money than you actually have in your bank account. However, if you haven't agreed this with your bank you could be charged for using your overdraft.

**Interest** – This can be a reward for saving money, or a charge for borrowing money, and is paid as a percentage called the interest rate.

**Debit** – Debit means the withdrawal of money from an account.

**Credit** – Credit is when you pay money into an account. If you buy something 'on credit', it means someone has lent you the money to pay for it.

**Credit rating** – Shops and agencies use this score to decide whether to lend you money.

**Bounced cheque** – If a bank refuses to pay a cheque because the person who wrote it doesn't have enough money to pay for it, this is known as a 'bounced cheque'.

cheque book and a cheque guarantee card, which allows you to pay for, and take away, things with a signed cheque. You'll receive a regular bank statement – usually every month – showing the amounts that have been paid in and withdrawn from your account and your overall balance.

### Cheque books and guarantee cards

A cheque book contains a number of cheques with your name on. The person you give a cheque to pays it into their bank account, and after a few days the money is taken (debited) from your account and added (or credited) to theirs. If you haven't got enough money in your current account to cover the value of the cheque you have written, the bank may refuse to honour your cheque and it will bounce. You may also be

given a cheque guarantee card. This guarantees that the bank will pay your cheque up to the amount stated on the card – usually £50 or £100. If there isn't enough money in your account to cover the value of the cheques you have written with your cheque guarantee card, you'll go overdrawn and may have to pay bank charges and interest. Strictly speaking, it is an offence to write a cheque when you know there is not enough money in your account to cover it, unless you have the permission of your bank to do so. Don't keep your cheque book and guarantee card together – if they are stolen this makes it easier to defraud you.

*Money can be withdrawn from ATM machines using a cash card*

### Cash cards

These allow you to take money out of your current account from a cash machine, using a confidential personal identification number (PIN). Never keep a record of this number with your cards; if someone finds them, it will be easy for them to access your money. If your PIN number is with the card and money is stolen from your account then your bank may not reimburse your money if they feel you have been negligent; always refer to the terms and conditions of your account. If your PIN number or card is stolen, contact your bank immediately.

## Debit cards

Your debit card allows you to buy things without writing a cheque or using cash. There is no legal age limit for obtaining a debit card, but as a rule banks tend to wait until their customers are 16 years old. You can also use it to pay for goods over the telephone or online. Your account is automatically debited with the amount you have spent. However, it can take a while (sometimes a few days) for payments to show on your balance. You can only go overdrawn with a debit card if you have the bank's agreement, otherwise you will be charged a fee. Many debit cards double as a cheque guarantee and cash card.

## Pre-paid cards

Pre-paid cards are growing in popularity in the UK, and are particularly targeted at under-18s and people with a poor credit rating. Users load the pre-paid card with a certain amount of money, and can only spend what they have on the card – this means it is impossible to go overdrawn on a pre-paid card. Most major card schemes (such as Visa, MasterCard and Maestro) now run pre-paid card schemes. Charges for cards vary greatly, although most charge a monthly fee.

## Savings accounts

A savings account normally provides a higher rate of interest than a current account. Most do not come with a cheque book or plastic card, and some have restrictions on when you can withdraw your money. For example, you may have to give between 30 and 60 days' notice before making a withdrawal. You will still be able to take out your money if you really have to, but will probably lose some of the extra interest you would earn if you left your money in the account. If you keep money in your savings account while you are overdrawn on your current account or have a loan, you may find the interest you are paying is higher than the interest that you earn on your savings account.

## What about tax on the interest I earn?

Interest earned on bank and building society accounts is usually paid after tax has been deducted from it. Unless you have a high income, that is normally the end of the matter, and there is no more tax to pay; see the tax section. If you are not a taxpayer (because your earnings are not high enough), you can either get the tax back by contacting a tax office or you can choose to have the interest paid to you without tax being deducted. Your bank or building society will have the forms for you to complete that allow them to do this.

---

## Don't be persuaded by offers or gifts if the services and charges are not as good as other banks or building societies

---

### What do I do if someone gives me a cheque?

Look to see that it is correctly written – that it is for the right amount, that it has been signed, and is not 'post-dated' (has a future date on). Pay the cheque into your account as soon as possible, using a paying-in slip. Banks do not usually accept cheques more than six months old.

## Credit

Credit is a way of buying goods by delaying the payment, or by paying in instalments. The different types of credit include loans, credit cards and store cards. You can find out more about loans in the next section.

### Credit cards

Credit cards are very useful, but can cause difficulties if too much money is borrowed. Young people must usually wait until they are 18 before they can have a credit card. Like debit cards, credit cards allow people to buy goods and services from a huge range of shops and other suppliers, in person, over the phone or on the Internet. Credit cards enable the shop to be paid straightaway, but the customer is not billed until sometime later. This means that the customer is being lent the money to buy the goods by the firm issuing the credit card. If you apply for a credit card, the firm issuing the card will check out your creditworthiness. A spending limit will be set on the account. A fee will be charged if you go over this, and the card may be cancelled. Each month you will receive a statement showing how much you have spent, how much is owed, and the minimum payment that must be made by a certain date. Ideally you should pay your bill in full to avoid being charged interest. If you make no payment at all, you will be charged a further penalty. Also your card could be cancelled and your credit rating could suffer. You can compare the costs of different cards by looking at the Annual Percentage Rate (APR), which is the rate of interest charged by the firm issuing the credit card. The lower the APR, the lower the cost of borrowing – the Financial Services Authority (FSA) website has a great tool to help you calculate these costs. Some types of borrowing on a credit card are more expensive than others. Using your credit card to withdraw cash can be more expensive than using it to buy goods.

### Store cards

These cards offer you credit when you buy goods at a particular store. You are sent a regular statement showing how much you have spent, and what you owe. You can pay a fixed minimum amount each time, with the rest being carried forward and appearing on your next statement. Interest is charged on the amount you haven't paid off. These charges are often higher than other types of credit card. You can check the store card's APR and compare it to your credit card.

## Borrowing

### Borrowing from a bank or building society

A bank or building society lends money either through allowing an overdraft or by making a loan.

### Overdrafts

A person becomes overdrawn when they spend more money than they have in their bank account. If you need to go overdrawn, you can usually arrange with your bank an authorised overdraft up to an agreed amount. Interest may be charged. The most expensive overdraft is an unauthorised one – which is run up without the agreement of the bank. Interest is paid on the amount overdrawn, and charges are added on top. If you ever find yourself in this situation, it is important to get in touch with the bank as soon as you can. Students may be offered interest-free overdrafts.

## Loans

A loan is an arrangement with your bank – or other financial institution – under which you are lent a specific amount of money. You enter into a contract for the loan. This will be at an agreed rate of interest and for a set period of time during which you repay the full loan. If you are under 18 it is very unlikely that you will be able to get a bank loan, as these kinds of contracts with 'minors' are not usually binding. All loans are different – always check the small print to see what you are signing up to.

## Buying goods by instalments – credit or hire purchase

You can often buy more expensive goods (e.g. cars, computers, TVs) by instalment – that is, by paying only part of the price at the time of purchase, and paying the rest later. Sometimes credit is available interest-free, but credit is normally an expensive way of paying for things. It is always a good idea to check the charges (the APR) that are being made. 'Hire purchase' is a special form of buying on credit. Technically the shop sells the goods to a finance company and you pay to 'hire' them over an agreed period. When you have paid off what you owe you make a final payment to purchase the goods (hence 'hire purchase'). Only then do you become the owner.

## Second thoughts

If you signed a credit deal at home (or away from the shop or business premises) you have a right to cancel if you act quickly. You will be sent a second copy of the agreement that will tell you how to cancel if you want to. You will have five days to do this.

## Getting into debt

People get into debt for all sorts of reasons. They may find they owe money to several different people and are tempted to borrow more to pay off some of these debts. This often becomes even more expensive. You know it's getting serious when you start getting badgered to make repayments by the people you owe money to – your 'creditors' – and you can't meet all the demands.

## What to do

⇨ Don't ignore the problem: it won't go away and will get worse the longer you leave it. You can get free help from a range of advice agencies.

⇨ Draw up a budget: list all the money you owe and the people to whom it is owed, what your income and reasonable living expenses are and see how much you can afford to pay back. There are a range of budgeting tools available online to help you do this. A useful budgeting tool is available on the FSA website, 'Money Made Clear'.

⇨ List your debts in their order of priority: at the top are those where non-payment can have really serious consequences – like losing your flat or home, having the electricity or gas cut off, or where non-payment is a criminal offence (like council tax and your TV licence). You should aim to pay these off first and then work out what's left over for the others, treating them equally.

⇨ Contact all your creditors: go and see them or write or phone; explain the position and show them your budget. Discuss with them what you can reasonably pay. Usually they will be prepared to negotiate. You may be able to agree to pay by instalments or, for a period of time, just to pay off the interest on your loan. If you are worried about contacting them directly you can contact a free advice agency for help.

⇨ Don't borrow more without getting advice: some individuals or companies lend money at very high rates of interest, making it difficult to keep up with repayments and hard to get out of debt.

## Help!

You can get help and advice from experts. Try the National Debtline or a Citizens Advice Bureau.

⇨ The above information is an extract from the document *My Money, My Rights*, produced by the Citizenship Foundation, and is reproduced by permission of John Murray (Publishers) Ltd. Visit www.citizenshipfoundation.org.uk for more information.

*© Hodder Murray 2009*

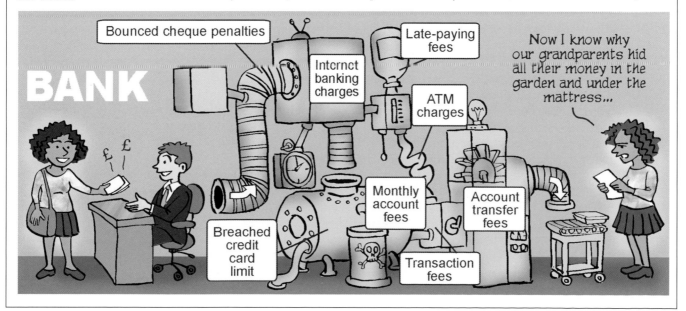

BANK

Bounced cheque penalties

Internet banking charges

Late-paying fees

ATM charges

Monthly account fees

Account transfer fees

Breached credit card limit

Transaction fees

Now I know why our grandparents hid all their money in the garden and under the mattress...

# How to be a prudent student

### Despite the economic climate, you can avoid getting into a credit crunch of your own at university

**By Harriet Swain**

What is the worst thing that can happen to you, financially speaking, in your first year at university? How about turning up for your first day, being asked to pay for your accommodation and finding your loan cheque hasn't arrived? And the second worst thing? Well, what about receiving your loan cheque, spending its contents, and then remembering you still owe rent?

Actually, there are loads of potential financial pitfalls that await you as a student, but these are probably the most common. And they are also two of the most preventable.

You can avoid the first by applying for support as early as possible. Like now, if you are in year 13. You don't have to wait until you have a firm offer of a place, or even until you are sure you want to start university this year. Just use your first-choice course and you can always change it later, or alter the start date if you decide you want to take a year out.

Go to the government website Student Finance England (studentfinance.direct.gov.uk) if you live in England. If you live elsewhere in the UK, you'll need to contact Student Finance Wales (studentfinancewales.co.uk), Student Finance Northern Ireland (studentfinanceni.co.uk) or the Student Awards Agency for Scotland (saas.gov.uk). Students from elsewhere in the European Union will need to look at the Directgov section of Student Finance England (studentfinance.direct.gov.uk) related to them, while international students can get information from the UK Council for International Student Affairs (ukcosa.org.uk).

Through these websites, you should be able to work out how much support you are likely to get and, if you have already applied for a higher education place, will be able to apply for this support online.

### Know your entitlements

Everyone is entitled to a loan that covers the full costs of fees which everyone has to pay. The fees will be £3,225 next year almost everywhere. The figure is likely to increase in future years, but the loan will only be repayable once you have finished and are earning more than £15,000 a year.

> **While 15% of all students surveyed chose universities where they could live at home, this was true of 27% of poorer students**

You are also entitled to a maintenance loan worth up to £4,950 a year if you are living away from home, and up to £6,928 if you are studying in London. The amount available depends on your household income but should be at least £3,564, unless you are living with parents. Again, it will be repayable only once you have left and are earning more than £15,000 a year.

If your household income – that is, your parents' income, unless you are a mature student – is below £50,020, you will be entitled to a maintenance grant. This is money that you don't need to pay back. The amount of grant depends on how close to £50,020 your household income is, and you get the full grant of £2,906 a year if your household income is £25,000 or

less. If you receive a grant, you may have the amount of maintenance loan available to you reduced.

*Accommodation will usually be the single biggest drain on a student's finances*

Some students, such as single parents or those with disabilities, are entitled to a special support grant of up to £2,906 depending on household income, instead of a maintenance grant. Disabled students are also eligible for disabled students allowances, which help cover the cost of specialist equipment, travel and help, while there are more grants for students with dependent children or other caring responsibilities.

It is also vital to check with individual universities or colleges about the scholarships and bursaries they offer. Many of these go unclaimed and they can be worth hundreds of pounds a year.

Six out of ten university applicants from lower socio-economic backgrounds surveyed by the National Union of Students claimed that the recession had affected their choice of course or institution this year. The survey, published last month, shows that while 15% of all students surveyed chose universities where they could live at home, this was true of 27% of poorer students.

One of the most expensive things you can do is drop out, so you shouldn't compromise too much on where and what you really want to study just because it seems to work out a bit cheaper. But it is certainly worth considering relative costs.

Paul Hammond, a second-year media and cultural studies student at Kingston University, says the higher cost of living down south meant he lost control of his spending in the first term. 'I'm from just near York and it's quite cheap there really,' he says. 'Here it was a bit of a culture shock.'

Stevie Wise, a third-year religious studies student at University of Glasgow started at Lancaster University, then moved to Glasgow, which she enjoys but has found much more expensive. 'When I was in Lancaster, it was £70 a week to live in halls but when I came here it was £100-plus,' she says. 'Had I known that, I might have made a different choice. On the other hand, in some cheaper areas it may be harder to find a part-time job.'

One option is to live at home, which is certainly much cheaper, although you'll need to take travel costs to the university into account. It can also prevent you getting some of the benefits of higher education, which include not only a good social life but learning to live independently and to budget.

According to Lynne Condell, chair of the Association of Student Money Advisers, working out a realistic budget before going to university is invaluable. Talk to other students and your parents about the sort of day-to-day expenses you can expect, and contact your course tutor to find out whether there are likely to be any course costs, such as trips, and whether you will need to buy particular books or pieces of equipment. Do this early and you could hit eBay or Amazon before the competition. If you do need to buy expensive equipment, such as a laptop, insure it.

Hammond recommends keeping up with your pre-university summer job as long as possible. Yes, it is nice to have a week or two seeing friends and being fussed over by mum before leaving the nest, but do the attractions of this outweigh the benefits of a couple of hundred pounds' extra in your pocket to spend on a wild student social life?

## Money in your pocket

Nor should you get so carried away by this social life that you forget to fix up paid employment for when you are at university. Most students do now take on some kind of job while they are studying, and if you leave it until you're desperate many of the best ones will have been snapped up. This is more the case than ever this year because of the recession, which means many traditional student jobs are going to non-students.

OK, so you've spent the summer sensibly budgeting, working and resisting the endless offers of credit and special deals that seem to arrive as soon as companies hear the word 'student'. Now you arrive at university and find you are suddenly thousands of pounds in the black. What do you do next?

'If you are 18 and someone pays £2,000 into your bank account, the temptation to go and blow it is enormous,' says Condell. She advises paying your rent, or putting money aside to pay it, before doing anything else. Then, keep an eye on your bank statements and be aware that regularly drawing out £10 or £20 in cash soon adds up.

Hammond knows the dangers. 'I vividly remember the day my flatmate came in and said the rent was coming out the next week,' he says. 'I went cold and thought there's no way I can afford to pay it.' Eventually, his parents bailed him out and he has curbed his spending, but it wasn't nice.

In addition to a maintenance loan of £1,948 this year and a maintenance grant of £945, plus another £1,000 a year grant from the university, he has two flexible part-time jobs, which together pay up to around £100 per week. He estimates that he spends about £60 a week on food, transport and one night out, while bills and his rent of £400 a month come on top.

He says it is important to ask for help early on rather than waiting until you are deeply in debt. In fact, ask for help even if you don't think you need it. During freshers' week, many universities offer to check that you are getting the right level of support and this can be invaluable. He assumed that his support was correct, but it turned out he had failed to fill in all the paperwork for the Student Loans Company and is due some extra. His housemate has just realised she is entitled to another £1,000 and could get another £1,000 to cover last year too.

His tip now for managing your money at university? 'Everything in moderation.'

12 May 2009

# Budgeting

## Information from Credit Action

### Help with budgeting

Every month, you should get a bank statement detailing all your transactions. This will include any interest or charges relating to your account and give you an up-to-date balance. Statements are normally issued automatically to you each month, but extra copies can be obtained by calling in, or phoning your branch (you may be charged a fee for this service), or using a cash machine that is linked to your bank or building society. However, an excellent way to keep up to date is to register for online banking by visiting your bank's website. Remember to dispose of old bank statements and other financial documents carefully by shredding them or cutting them up thoroughly. You don't want your fun at university being spoilt by identity theft!

Budgeting is the art of keeping your spending under control – but this is not necessarily as simple as it sounds! However, the time you spend planning your budget for the coming year will be time well spent.

As a budget has to be accurate to be effective you need to keep track of everything you spend. Therefore, it is important to monitor your spending even when you buy everyday things at the supermarket, the pub or the kebab shop.

These small items soon add up – and it is likely that you will spend more on them than you think. One very easy way to budget as you go today is by using the all new Credit Action 'Spendometer'. You can download this for free from www.creditaction.org. uk/Spendometer, allowing you to budget easily with your mobile phone.

In conjunction with this you need to try and record accurately what you have spent using cheques (writing on stubs makes this easy) together with debit and credit cards (your bank does the work for you with your statements!). You should then have a clear picture of your spending.

### Why budget?

Budgeting may seem dull, but there are several really good reasons to budget:

1 It gives you an accurate picture of your financial situation.
2 It could well enable you to reduce your spending as you identify certain areas where you are spending too much, and thus improve your overall position.
3 It will show you (and your parents and bank manager!) that you are handling your money wisely.
4 It prevents you running up substantial debt on which you will have to pay interest and which you will have to repay!

### When you budget

#### 1. Be absolutely honest

There is no point budgeting if, for example, you put down nothing for coffees, text messages or magazines! Keep track using the 'Spendometer' as you go along.

#### 2. Look at your priorities

When you have first produced your budget, look at what you are spending your money on. Does it accurately reflect your priorities?

Accommodation will be your largest expenditure. If you are in halls of residence be sure to pay the residential fees at the beginning of the term. If you are in outside rented accommodation you could set up a standing order to pay the rent monthly.

However, do ensure that there is sufficient money in your account each month – banks don't like it when you go overdrawn without arranging it beforehand or exceed an agreed overdraft limit! Because of the extra work involved in having to 'bounce' a cheque or stop payment of a standing order they will make additional charges to your account.

Your individual priorities may vary, but it is essential you have food and drink, accommodation, warmth and light. Therefore ensure you always set aside enough to pay for:

⇨ basic foodstuffs;
⇨ rent;
⇨ gas/electricity.

If you are house-sharing, you will need to come to an arrangement with your house mates about how to pay for bills and food. For example, you might all agree to pay into a shared pot for food, rent and gas and electricity or all shop separately but share the cost of bills and essentials like milk and bread. Different people work differently but communication is key to reaching an agreement that suits you all. It is vital to establish practical priorities in your spending.

#### 3. Pay by instalments

Utility charges mount up and your quarterly bills can be much higher than you probably anticipate. For these regular bills it might be easier to spread your payments over the year paying by direct debit monthly – but again, do ensure that you keep enough money in your account to meet these debits as they arrive each month. The gas or electricity company may even offer you a discount for paying by direct debit!

The more you can organise bills to come on a monthly basis the less likely you'll be facing an unexpected or forgotten bill appearing suddenly. Spreading payments over time will also help you budget. If you are struggling to pay for any items you must get in touch with whoever you owe money to straightaway. Do not be afraid of seeking help from your union representative or welfare officer at college.

#### 4. Keep your spending disciplined

Use your budget to guide your spending. Stick to the shopping lists you produce, set yourself limits on the 'Spendometer', and try to minimise 'impulse' spending. If you struggle with this it often helps to watch fewer adverts on TV, read fewer magazines or go to the shops less often.

#### 5. Review your budget

When you have first finished your

budget, review it carefully. Go over it again:
⇨ Are you sure there is nothing missing?
⇨ Do you want to alter your spending habits in any way?
⇨ Have you got your priorities right?

### How to budget

#### 1. Take it seriously
Managing our money isn't an exciting thing to think about and yet it's absolutely crucial to learn to do it well, not just for when you're a student, but for our lives in general.

When money is tight, as it will be while you are at university, you need to learn how to make your limited resources go a long way.

#### 2. Spread income
You should try to spread your income over the whole period to which it relates. If you receive your loan cheque at the beginning of a term, remember that it has to last the whole term! Don't be tempted to spend it all at once – expenses will keep on coming!

#### 3. Spend sensibly
This is essential – remember that money for tomorrow's needs is more important than today's wants. Sometimes this will mean going without things you'd like to have, like that third pint, the new DVD, that frothy *latte* or the nightly kebab on the way home from the pub, but in the long run cutting these things out could save you a lot of difficulties. Try to take advantage of student offers such as those available with your NUS card or from www.studentbeans.com

#### 4. Work out your spending
When calculating your budget you need to work out your income (the amount of money you have coming in) and expenditure (the amount of money you have going out) on a regular basis – monthly is ideal. For example, if you get a cheque for £600 which is supposed to last you three months, allocate £200 for each of those months as your income. Similarly, if you have a quarterly phone bill of £60 allocate £20 to each month's expenditure. Standing orders and direct debits are a helpful way of doing this.

#### 5. Drawing up a budget (also known as a financial statement)
Many items go into a budget and to help you out an example is given on the next page.

#### 6. Analysing your budget
Once you have completed your budget and added up the totals, how does it look? Hopefully, you will be in a position of showing a surplus (some money left over), however small.

If you have less money than you need, according to your budget, this is called a deficit. If this is the case, don't panic! There are things that you can do to improve your position.

#### 7. Ways of improving your budget position
⇨ Try to trim your spending in non-essential areas. For example, you can do this by avoiding situations where you know you're more likely to spend, like window shopping, and by being disciplined in writing up shopping lists and sticking to them instead of just seeing what you fancy when you get to the supermarket.
⇨ See if you can get a holiday job to boost your income. Contact a local employment agency, look out for signs in local shops and businesses, or search the Internet. If getting a job is viable, try to apply as early as possible and ideally aim to earn enough to repay any debts you may have accumulated during the academic year. By doing so you will be starting a new academic year debt free (except for your student loan of course!). This is a great thing to aim for.
⇨ Try to cut out paying excess interest. You can do this by:
(a) taking advantage of the free overdraft and other facilities offered by your bank or building society.
(b) ensuring that if you have done this already you are borrowing as cheaply as you can. This will almost certainly mean continuing to borrow from your bank or building society within agreed limits. The advantages of this can be seen in the table below. It shows the approximate Annual Percentage Rate (APR*) of interest that you would be charged to borrow from various organisations.

* APR – whenever you are using credit it is vital that you compare these rates as well as the 'cash' price. A high APR can make goods cost much more than you would imagine. Use one of the calculators on www.moneybasics.co.uk to help you.

### Personal budget
It is a great idea to keep a running budget. One popular way to do this is to use a spreadsheet. Visit www.creditaction.org.uk/student for an Excel Student Budget Sheet. Try to keep your budget up to date by spending a few minutes once a month going through it. That way you'll always be informed and in control of your financial situation – it should take no more than half an hour – pretty much painless!

⇨ The above information is an extract from the document *Moneymanual for students: get clued up, stay quids in!* and is reprinted with kind permission from Credit Action. Visit www.creditaction.org.uk for more information.

© Credit Action

### Borrowing table

| Lender | Typical rates of interest |
|---|---|
| 1. Banks/Building Societies | |
| (a) special student packages with agreed initial borrowing limit | Nil |
| (b) any increase over agreed limit negotiated with your bank | 5%-8% |
| (c) any unauthorised borrowing – beware! | 20%-30% |
| 2. Finance houses | 11%-16% |
| 3. Credit cards | 10%-20% |
| 4. Credit unions | 10%-27% |
| 5. Store cards | 15%-30% |
| 6. Licensed 'non-standard' lenders | 50%-200% |
| 7. Illegal money lenders (loan sharks) – AVOID! | Whatever they can get away with |

Source: 'Moneymanual for students: get clued up, stay quids in!', Credit Action.

## Sample monthly personal budget sheet

### INCOME

| Loan/grant/bursary | |
|---|---|
| Support from family | |
| Part-time job | |
| Other | |

TOTAL MONTHLY INCOME: _____

TOTAL MONTHLY EXPENDITURE: _____

BALANCE (monthly income less monthly expenditure): _____

MONTHLY SURPLUS/(DEFICIT): _____

### EXPENDITURE

| Formal commitments | Rent | | | Chemist | |
|---|---|---|---|---|---|
| | Water | | | Public transport | |
| | Service charge | | | Sports/hobbies | |
| | Insurance | | | Videos/DVDs/CDs | |
| | Electricity | | | Alcohol/drinks | |
| | Gas | | | Cigarettes | |
| | Phone/mobile/Internet | | | Other | |
| | TV rental | | If you have a car | Fuel | |
| | TV licence | | | Servicing/maintenance (allow for new tyres) | |
| If you have a car | Road tax | | | Parking | |
| | Insurance | | Occasional costs | Christmas | |
| | MOT certificate | | | Birthdays | |
| | Residents' parking permit | | | Holidays | |
| Everyday spending | Food | | | Subscriptions | |
| | Toiletries | | | Clothing | |
| | Books/stationery | | | Trips out | |
| | Newspapers/magazines | | | Meals out | |
| | Photocopying/printer ink/toner cartridges | | | Balls | |
| | Launderette | | | Graduation costs | |

Source: 'Moneymanual for students: get clued up, stay quids in!'. Credit Action.

# Student income and expenditure 2007/08

## Information from the Department for Innovation, Universities and Skills

The latest survey outlining students' income, spending and saving has been published today by the Department for Innovation, Universities and Skills. This survey looks at students' financial situations under both the new and old financial support systems, and compares these with the previous survey (2004/05).

For first year full-time students the survey showed that:

⇨ The average expenditure of undergraduate students in their first year of study has increased by 12 per cent since 2004/05.

⇨ This was driven by an increase of 68 per cent in the cost of participating in Higher Education – mainly due to the introduction of variable fees in 2006.

⇨ More than 80 per cent of students consider the long-term benefits of higher education outweigh the costs and that they will ultimately earn more as a result.

⇨ Students' incomes increased in line with this – up by 15 per cent since 2004/05 due to the new student support package, including the tuition fee loan.

⇨ Increased financial support means that students are relying less on family and paid work for income.

⇨ First year students are less likely to combine work with their studies; the proportion working during term time dropped from 58 per cent to 49 per cent.

⇨ In a change from the previous survey, average student income is similar across all social groups.

⇨ Students in their first year receiving the new support are expected to finish for the summer with a net debt of £3,500. This compares with an average student debt of £7,800 for those completing their courses in 2007/08.

David Lammy, Minister of State for Higher Education, said:

'Higher education remains one of the best pathways to a rewarding career, and it is good to see that students recognise it as a good investment for their future, a fact also seen in the record numbers of applications to university.

'This government continues to invest more than ever in higher education and we firmly believe that finance should never be a barrier to good education. This is why we continue to make generous loans and grants available to students, and

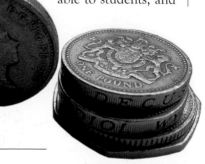

www.independence.co.uk

universities themselves provide bursaries to students who have genuine need of them.

'Today's survey shows that the overwhelming majority of students from all backgrounds still consider the benefits of higher education to outweigh the costs. In an increasingly competitive world, we also know that employers are aware of the range of skills that graduates can bring to their businesses.'

Since the previous student survey, carried out in 2004/05, new levels of student support have been introduced. For 2009/10 this includes:

⇨ maintenance grants of up to £2,906, which are targeted at students from lower income backgrounds;

⇨ tuition fee loans of up to £3,225, meaning students no longer have to pay their fees up-front.

⇨ These loans do not have to be repaid until students have left university and have an annual salary in excess of £15,000; and,

⇨ all those students receiving a maximum grant could also receive a bursary from their university. This was typically £800 in 2008/09.

Claire Johnson, Principal Research Fellow at the Institute for Employment Studies and one of the report authors, said:

'Student income has risen overall, although the majority of the increase is driven by income from tuition fee loans, which are paid directly to the students' institutions.

'Government grants and loans are playing a more important role for students studying under the new financial support system. If we compare first year students in 2007/08 with first years in 2004/05, we see that they are more reliant on these sources and less reliant on financial support from their parents or income from paid work.'

---

### The average expenditure of undergraduate students in their first year of study has increased by 12 per cent since 2004/05

---

Government funding for higher education has risen for 2009/10, with funding for 30,000 more students than in 2007/08. There have also been efforts to help both businesses and individuals during the downturn, with more than 70 universities and colleges investing £27 million in extra courses and internships across the country.

### Further information

1 The survey is carried out every two to three years.

2 The 2007/08 survey was jointly commissioned by the Department for Innovation, Universities and Skills (DIUS) and the Welsh Assembly Government (WAG).

3 It was conducted in partnership by the National Centre for Social Research (NatCen) and the Institute for Employment Studies (IES), and presents the findings for students from England.

4 A separate report covers students from Wales (whose income and expenditure patterns are very similar).

5 The 2007/08 survey covers both full-time and part-time students at higher education institutions (HEI) and further education colleges (FEC), including the Open University (OU), participating in undergraduate courses during the 2007/08 academic year.

6 Data were collected between January and March 2008 via face-to-face interviews with a randomly selected sample of 2,686 full-time and part-time English-domiciled students at 80 institutions in England and Wales. Students also completed a seven-day expenditure diary.

---

### More than 80 per cent of students consider the long-term benefits of higher education outweigh the costs

---

7 'Net debt' is the sum of outstanding student loan and other borrowing (e.g. overdrafts, commercial credit, informal loans), less savings.

*21 April 2009*

⇨ The above information is reprinted with kind permission from the Department for Innovation, Universities and Skills. Visit www.dius.gov.uk for more information.

© Crown copyright

# Young, jobless, broke: today's lost generation

**Unable to buy their own home, saddled with student debt and struggling to find work, the class of 2009 could have their lives scarred for years by the credit crunch**

Back in the carefree days of the Noughties boom, Britain's youngsters were swept along by the buy-now-pay-later culture embraced by consumers up and down the country. During a decade of near-full employment, many skipped nimbly from one job – and one credit card – to another, and rainy days were such a distant memory that they hardly seemed worth saving for.

But with the supply of cheap credit drying up and a generation of school and university leavers about to flood the recession-hit job market, thousands of young people with no memory of the early 1990s recession are shocked into the realisation that the world of 2009 is very different.

## An alarming 18.3% of 16- to 25-year-olds are unemployed

Katie Orme, 19, who lives in Birmingham, says she has decided never to get a credit card after seeing the problems that her parents and 22-year-old sister have had with debt – just one of the hard lessons that she has had to learn.

Orme finished her A-levels a year ago, and has been searching for a job – and living at home with her parents – ever since. She has had to sign on to support herself and is now on a 12-week internship at the Prince's Trust to improve her CV. The trust says that the number of calls from anxious people such as Orme has shot up by 50% over six months.

'It's so hard to get a job at the moment,' she says, 'it's better to go and get more qualifications so when more jobs are available you will be better suited.'

**By Heather Stewart and Kathryn Hopkins**

She is far from alone in trimming her expectations to fit a credit-crunched world: many youngsters who have seen nothing like the current turmoil have been shocked into changing their outlook. A recent survey by Post Office financial services found that most 16 to 24 year olds believe that it will take a decade for their living standards to return to pre-crisis levels – and almost half have been jolted into cutting back their use of credit cards.

The number of under-25s out of work and claiming Jobseeker's Allowance has increased by more than 200,000, to 456,000, over the past year, according to the latest government figures released last week. On the wider labour market survey measure, an alarming 18.3% of 16 to 25 year olds are unemployed.

Brendan Barber, the TUC general secretary, says: 'Youth unemployment is at its highest rate for 15 years. Unemployment leaves a permanent scar on young people's lives and the government must do all it can to stop joblessness blighting another generation.'

David Blanchflower, the labour market expert who recently stepped down from the Bank of England's monetary policy committee, says that even short periods of unemployment can have a long-term 'scarring' effect, affecting people's job prospects for many years.

'It's a bit like male metalworkers from Sheffield in the 1980s – it continues for ever,' he says. He believes unemployment among the young has become a 'national crisis' and has lobbied Gordon Brown to act. 'This is going to be the biggest issue in the next election. The danger is that we have a lost generation.'

And, unlike the many thousands of manufacturing lay-offs during the 1980s recessions, he says, a wide swathe of social groups will be hit this time, from working-class school

leavers to middle-class students. 'It's a call to arms for their parents and their grandparents,' he says. 'We need to get all parties together and say, what are we going to do about this?'

David Willetts, the Conservative shadow skills secretary, is demanding public funding for young people chucked off apprenticeships by cash-strapped firms, and extra places at further education and in postgraduate training, to ease the 'pressure points' caused by the recession. 'The risk is that young people find themselves on the dole for months, if not years, and in the long run, their life-time earnings are depressed,' he says.

Joe Phillips, who is 24, followed in the footsteps of tens of thousands of other graduates and spent time travelling abroad. 'I didn't see it as a frantic rush to get on the career path,' he says.

However, when he moved to London in September 2008 to try to find a job in the media, he regretted his decision not to enter the jobs market as soon as he had graduated.

'I struggled to find any paid work,' he says. 'I wanted to do communications for a charity but ended up doing a free internship and then a low-paid job.' During this period, he had to sleep on friends' sofas and at his sister's flat to make ends meet. At one point, things were so bad he had to move back to the West Midlands to live with his parents.

He has now returned to London, filling a temporary job at the Parkinson's Disease Society which he hopes will be made permanent – but he is acutely aware that nothing is certain in the current climate.

Gerwyn Davies, public policy adviser at the Chartered Institute of Personnel and Development (CIPD), believes that the job situation facing today's young people is worse than any generation has seen for decades.

'It's a very difficult pill for young people to swallow,' he says. 'We already have a situation where one in six young people are unemployed. Unfortunately, this situation is going to worsen.'

He points out that they will have to compete against a growing pool of more experienced workers who

have lost their jobs: 'They will have qualifications, but won't have the same work experience as other people coming on to the claimant count.'

A recent report by the CIPD revealed that nearly half of the employers it surveyed were not planning to recruit school leavers or graduates this summer. For many young adults hit by the downturn, who are relying on the generosity of parents or claiming state benefits, the normal process of growing up has been delayed: 35 is the new 25.

While many who came of age in the 1990s were able to buy a home with a 95% or 100% mortgage and reap the windfall as it tripled in value – or, for the luckiest, stroll into a job in the City and join the ranks of the super-rich – today the concerns of many are the more prosaic ones of finding work and earning enough to pay the bills.

Phillips says there is a big difference between young people ten years ago and his contemporaries: 'We have different priorities. I'm just trying to pin down a permanent job and pay the rent. Buying a house and starting a family seems like a distant thing.'

Wes Streeting, president of the National Union of Students, fears that graduates emerging from university this year will fare even worse than Phillips and his cohorts. He calls the Class of 2009 'generation crunch'.

'They're the first to pay top-up tuition fees of £3,000 a year, and

are graduating into the worst labour market for a very long time,' he says.

Labour has already announced a number of measures to help: Alistair Darling promised in the budget that young people would be guaranteed a job or training place. However, with cash tight, this promise only applies to those who have already been searching for work for 12 months and Streeting says that's far too long to wait.

'The government needs to look again at the situation facing graduates and what they can do proactively to ensure they are not sitting around becoming depressed and disgruntled because they're unable to get a job,' he says.

When top-up tuition fees of up to £3,000 a year were introduced, ministers cited the hefty increase in earning power that a degree brings, but Streeting says that argument looks much weaker in a tough economic climate. The NUS has just launched a campaign to replace the fees by a tax, which would be levied as a percentage of graduates' earnings, hitting the highly paid hardest. 'The current economic climate shows the futility of our funding system for higher education,' he adds.

With jobs hard to find, young people are increasingly putting their lives on hold. The National Association of Estate Agents said last week that almost seven out of ten would-be first-time buyers have now given up hope of ever owning their own home.

Instead of branching out on their own, a growing number of youngsters are sharing rental properties. A recent report by flatshare website SpareRoom.co.uk showed that there were 143,000 more people living in a flat or house share in the UK in May 2009 than in autumn 2007, when the credit crunch first began to make itself felt. The UK population of flatsharers has swelled to 2.8 million as renters abandon living alone to save money during the crisis.

For many, the 'bank of mum and dad' is the only one whose doors are still open. In the Post Office survey, almost 60% of 18 to 24 year olds polled said they were living rent-free with their parents.

Paul Mullins, chief executive of National Debtline, says: 'Young people face various unique challenges that do not affect other age groups in the same way. Often they have a large amount of student debt and are often looking to move out of home for the first time. Quite often young people are on a low income, they are at the start of their careers so their earning power is not as high as older age groups.'

And it's not just spending habits that have changed: Orme says that the credit crunch has forced her to put other key life decisions on hold as well. 'I can't hold down a relationship or look after a child with no money,' she says. 'There's no point in bringing a child into the world if you haven't got the money to look after it.'

Even for those who have managed to find a job, recession has made things more tricky. 'Unless something changes dramatically, I can't see myself

doing all three,' Joanna Williams, who is 25, says of buying a house, getting married and having a baby. 'I know people who have chosen to have a baby and not get married because it's too expensive to do both.'

She believes that she will never be able to get a foot on the property ladder: 'I remember when I was leaving school I was told I wouldn't own a house because they were too expensive, and now I think that it will never happen because of mortgages. If you want a house by 30, it would be something that you would have to sacrifice everything else for.'

She believes that the tradition of parents helping their children financially with weddings and buying houses is becoming less common as recession bites. 'A lot of us would be reluctant to ask our parents for help because we don't know how stable their finances are.' Williams has been working as a PA for a broadcasting

company for a year and would like to move on, but the recession has made her fear taking risks to pursue her dream career.

'One of the things is that my job is stable and it's a continuing contract, but because of the way things are it makes me reluctant to move on because I am lucky to have a job. I don't want to take any risks.'

There have been some tentative signs of green shoots in the UK over recent weeks and some economists have bravely begun to suggest that we may be at the end of the beginning.

But even if they are right, the impact of this 21st-century recession will last for many years. Just as the hardship of postwar rationing taught a generation of Britons to waste not, want not, grow their own and make ends meet, today's youngsters are learning tough lessons that will last a lifetime.
*21 June 2009*
© *Guardian News & Media Ltd 2009*

# Two-thirds of teens demand better financial education

### Information from Abbey

⇨ *Abbey and Citizenship Foundation launch guide to advise teenagers on financial and consumer rights.*
⇨ *65% of teenagers think further education is not necessarily worth getting into debt for.*

Leading high street bank Abbey has joined up with educational charity, Citizenship Foundation to call for greater education for 14 to 18 year olds on how to manage their money. The call to action comes after a poll revealed over two thirds of teenagers (70%) would like to be taught more about finance at school. With 57% of respondents worrying about money and 41% unaware as to the consequences of being overdrawn, there is a clear need for greater financial education in UK schools. As a result, Abbey has partnered with the Citizenship Foundation to create the *My Money, My Rights* guide for teenagers which contains simple tips and advice

on organising finances.

The national poll of 3,000 14 to 18 year olds reveals that 65% of 14 to 18 year olds feel that additional qualifications are not necessarily worth getting into debt for. However, further education finance is one of the three topics that respondents said they would like to learn more on at school (37%) – in addition to budgeting (48%) and tax (41%), indicating that students want to hear more in these areas and to make more informed decisions.

John Thorpe, Retail Director, Abbey, commented: 'It's no surprise that this age group is calling for more education in this area and as a

bank, we recognise the importance of providing financial information which will enable people to make informed choices about how they manage their money. It's never been

more important for young people to have a grasp of financial and economic matters and it's a real worry that four out of five 14 to 18 year olds have little or no understanding of the current economic crisis.'

Tony Breslin, Chief Executive, Citizenship Foundation: 'Having a grasp of our economic and financial rights and responsibilities has never been more important. It is vital to build a broader understanding of the world around us, and to lay the foundations for greater participation and better decision-making or as we put it, effective citizenship.'

The research also reveals a gender divide. Girls are more likely to ask family members for guidance on their finances (65% vs. 46%) whereas boys are happier to approach a teacher (20% vs. 6%). Teenagers from Swansea and Glasgow are most

likely to recognise they need financial education, with 87% and 84% stating they would like to learn more about managing their finances at school. This is compared to Dublin, with only 28% of teenagers highlighting that they would like greater understanding in this area.

The *My Money, My Rights* guide has been inspired by the Citizenship Foundation's award winning *Young Citizen's Passport*. It covers a range of issues that impact teenagers' lives, including banks and building societies, consumer law and student finance, providing concise, easy to use advice on everything from what to do if you get into debt to avoiding Internet scams. Two lesson plans have been developed alongside the guide to help teachers introduce managing money and the guide effectively into the classroom.

Financial inclusion and capability is one of seven priorities for the Abbey Corporate Social Responsibility programme which funds financial education and money advice in the communities in which Abbey operates. This work, alongside staff volunteering programmes to run one-day learning experiences in schools, is helping to raise levels of numeracy and combat financial exclusion.

The *My Money, My Rights* guide and accompanying lesson plans can be downloaded from www.aboutabbey.com and www.citizenshipfoundation.org.uk
6 March 2009

⇨ The above information is reprinted with kind permission from Abbey. Visit www.aboutabbey.com for more information.
© *Abbey*

# Money talks

### The TES talks to schools who are taking action and helping pupils understand money

Last week was celebration time for 27-year-old Gemma. After six years of full-time work as a PR consultant, she managed to pay off the £10,000 bank loan she'd bought as a student. The loan, charging double-digit interest, was sold to Gemma by the high street bank that she'd saved with since she was a child.

'I know it sounds stupid, but at the time I didn't even look at how much interest I was paying, or how long it

### By Madeleine Brettingham

would take me to be debt free,' she says. 'Since the bank was offering it to me I thought I must be able to pay it back and just looked at it as free money – a sort of top-up for my student loan.'

This might sound naive. But Gemma isn't stupid. She's a smart, hard-working young woman who

allowed herself to be manipulated by an industry that is all too happy to exploit consumer ignorance of its products. She's not alone. A study in 2007 by one personal finance organisation found that half of young people were in debt by the age of 17 – a statistic that's even more alarming in view of the global credit crisis.

### A study in 2007 by one personal finance organisation found that half of young people were in debt by the age of 17

Being financially savvy has never been more important. The UK is marching steadily into a recession of the like not seen in a generation, and British households have amassed record levels of debt. According to credit-rating agency Standard & Poor's, a drop in house prices sent

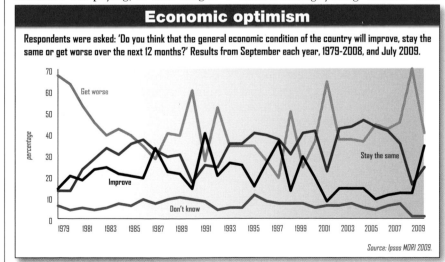

**Economic optimism**

Respondents were asked: 'Do you think that the general economic condition of the country will improve, stay the same or get worse over the next 12 months?' Results from September each year, 1979-2008, and July 2009.

Get worse · Stay the same · Improve · Don't know

Source: Ipsos MORI 2009.

600,000 homeowners into negative equity last year. Our financial literacy is a national embarrassment according to a report from the Organisation for Economic Co-operation and Development, which concluded that Britons systematically overestimated their knowledge of money matters. A study by the Financial Services Authority the same year showed that seven per cent of people even had trouble reading a bank statement. 'About half of people don't take account of the interest rate when they're borrowing or saving,' says Vyvian Bronk, head of financial capability at the FSA. 'People's ability in this area is not even close to what we assume.'

Last year Ed Balls, the Secretary of State for Children, Schools and Families, introduced a £11.5 million scheme to boost financial education in schools, giving pupils the tools to make smart choices about their future.

The My Money project, which runs until 2011, will develop resources to improve financial literacy, launch a dedicated My Money week this July, and field a network of regional consultants to help schools and local authorities find time for financial training in a crowded curriculum.

A department spokesman called it, 'the first project to provide joined-up financial education starting from when a child first starts school, through to the age of 19'. The Government has also taken the step of making economic wellbeing and financial capability part of the programme of study for Personal Social and Health Education, and in Scotland the Scottish Centre for Financial Education provides help and advice to teachers.

But how do you make the dry world of annual percentage rates and balance transfers accessible to pupils? Wendy van den Hende, chief executive of the Personal Finance Education Group (PFEG), which leads the My Money project, says, 'It's a useful way to teach other stuff children are interested in, such as ethical investment, the environment and fair trade. Most will have mobile phones and part-time jobs. It's about helping them to develop financial acumen, enabling them to challenge and question, not just telling them don't get into debt.'

Big, fun practical activities can help the subject come alive, like the stock market day held by PFEG at Lawrence Sheriff School in Rugby. Year 9s were given £100,000 to invest on an impromptu trading floor staged in the school's main hall, and relayed news flashes and investment updates on to a screen using software called Stock Market Challenge. Between them, pupils had to act as investment managers, media analysts and traders, and the winning group was the one with the best-performing portfolio.

It's not exactly an exercise in financial prudence, but Laura Kisby, head of careers and enterprise, believes it taught pupils about risk. 'It showed them that on the stock market, even if you make a wise decision, things can get out of control. Pupils also learnt how to read and make sense of financial articles, and 71 per cent said it had improved their negotiating skills,' she says.

With such a complex subject, it's no wonder most schools wait until secondary level before broaching it, but it is possible to start as early as reception. At St George the Martyr C of E Primary School in Camden, London, staff teach the value of money to children as young as four by getting them to set up imaginary shoe shops and price their own goods.

The school council is also in charge of parts of the school budget – poring over electricity and stationery bills in order to cut costs. In maths class, older pupils calculate how much energy they can save by switching the lights off, while Year 1 children count the sheets of paper they've used, and how much it has cost the school.

Amanda Szewczyk-Radley, headteacher, says: 'They're interested in the environment anyway, so it ticks a lot of boxes, and at this rate it looks like they'll save thousands.

'I've told them they can spend this money any way they want to improve school environment. They've been talking about getting a pond, and it's been a great motivator.'

The fact is, children might be more interested in money than we think – 90 per cent of teenagers think about it on a daily basis according to PFEG. To spark their interest, it's a case of approaching the subject in a way that chimes with their daily lives.

Su Kler, an Advanced Skills Teacher at Salesian College, an independent Catholic boys' school in Farnborough, uses her maths lessons to help pupils pick a mobile phone contract. 'Because it's not ordinary maths, it's really easy to get their interest,' she says. 'You'd be surprised how much some of them know.'

Su admits that pupils' financial skills aren't always as polished as they ought to be, however. 'I did a quiz and one of them thought a mortgage was someone who worked on the motorway,' she says. 'Now there is more pressure to have the right trainers, the right gadgets, I think people are less sensible about money than they used to be.'

This is why children need to be taught, not just the names and purposes of financial products, but basic money sense, according to Martin Lewis, of www.moneysavingexpert. com. The consumer champion says children need to be taught a healthy scepticism of banks and big business in order to make the right decisions. 'Their job is to make money from you – not that there's anything wrong with that, but it's the reality. The last place you should go to for financial advice is your bank, because it will try to sell you products.'

Children need to be taught about debt – how banks will try to sell you loans over a long period to maximise their interest – and educated in the difference between good borrowing (a cheap, government-approved student loan) and bad borrowing (expensive credit cards). It will mean people, like Gemma, don't just fall into debt. And the impact on the broader economy could be huge: 'If we'd had decent financial lessons in schools ten to 12 years ago we wouldn't be in the mountain of debt we are now,' he says.

Unsurprisingly, Martin isn't a fan of banks getting involved in financial education – 'disgusting sham branding, we shouldn't let them bring their own agenda into schools', he says. However, many schools use resources provided by high street names, and the PFEG receives much of its funding from the industry. A lot of the help and advice schools have access to is bankrolled by brands such as HSBC and Barclays. So does this mean teachers should try and steer clear of their products?

The answer is probably to pick and choose, and realise that resources provided by banks, while useful up to a point, are unlikely to be written from a sceptical consumer-led perspective. HSBC, whose What Money Means scheme run in conjunction with PFEG has worked with primaries in eight regions across the country, says that it is aware of concerns, but would never advertise to children.

Peter Bull, head of HSBC in the Community, says, 'We don't put the logo on anything that goes in front of pupils and we stress to staff that go into schools that they shouldn't be talking about HSBC. It would be ridiculous for us to do that. We want more financially educated people. It's good for the public, and it's in the interests of the institution.'

Teaching about finance can be daunting, but knowing where to go for help is the first step. The PFEG website (www.pfeg.org.uk) or the Scottish Centre for Financial Education run by Learning and Teaching Scotland (www.ltsscotland. org.uk/financialeducation) are good places to start, and the personal finance section of www.teachernet. gov.uk also has some useful links.

In England, the Government recommends teaching the basics of counting, shopping and spending at key stages 1 and 2, the workings of banks and big business at KS3, and a bit of extra nitty gritty about debt and wages at KS4 – blending it with other subjects such as maths, English and technology. Who knows, you might even pick up a few tips.

Mike Simpson, head of RE, citizenship and PSHE at the Venerable Bede C of E School in Sunderland teaches Year 8s about money management using a holiday budgeting CDRom called 'Lifeskills – Traveller's Cheque'. He admits: 'I'm not very good with money and this has helped me a great deal. I didn't have any financial education at school – none – so I've found it as interesting as the pupils.'

But does finance education actually work? There's no point in throwing millions at the problem, not to mention the nights spent cobbling together resources, if pupils just leave school and make the same mistakes as their parents.

Mick Mcateer, director of the Financial Inclusion Centre, a not-for-profit think-tank, and a former policy adviser at Which?, says: 'Everyone supports it, it's like motherhood and apple pie, but there's not a lot of research about it. It's problematic because with schemes that start today it could be a generation before they pay dividends.'

Professor Nigel Waites, director of the Financial Services Research Forum at Nottingham University, agrees. 'It's not liable to be remedied by a quick fix. Part of the problem is the industry is so complex. And also, let's be honest, most people find it inherently dull.' Dean Karlan, a professor of economics at Yale University, delivers a more brutal verdict: 'The best evidence on impact of compulsory financial education in schools in America shows a big fat no effect,' he says.

There is also scepticism from some quarters about whether PFEG's approach of spreading financial education across the curriculum is the right one. Rod McKee, head of financial capability at the ifs School of Finance, an education charity that trains pupils in 300 schools, says that incorporating the subject into other curriculum areas such as maths is unwise. 'Maths teachers are teaching concepts, but while it might be helpful to know the formula for compound interest, pupils need to understand the consequences,' he says, pointing to a Ofsted report last year that said spreading the subject across the curriculum led to fragmented experiences for pupils. The school wants finance education to be offered as a stand-alone subject, like modern languages, that all schools must provide. But, in a pressurised timetable, a cross-curricular approach is better than nothing.

Families can set a good example to children by giving them a weekly allowance, involving them in the family budget, and not bailing them out when they've overspent. As Niall Ferguson, the historian, writes, in his new book *The Ascent of Money*, 'It's a well-established fact that a substantial proportion of the general public in the English-speaking world is ignorant of finance.' With the public's financial literacy in such a state, school may be the only place pupils can learn from their parents' mistakes.

*16 January 2009*
© *Times Educational Supplement (TES)*

# KEY FACTS

⇨ 2009 GDP growth in developing countries is expected to fall to 4.5% from 7.9% in 2007. As many as 90 million more people could be trapped in extreme poverty – living on less than $1.25 a day. (page 1)

⇨ The Bank of England base rate, as high as 5.75% in July 2007, has been slashed over the following 18 months, hitting just 0.5% in March 2009. (page 4)

⇨ A single adult with no children now needs to earn at least £13,900 a year before tax to reach the minimum living standard. This is a £500 rise from 2008; nearly half of this extra income is needed for the rising cost of food. (page 6)

⇨ Household expenditure fell by one per cent in the last quarter of 2008 – the biggest fall since 1980 – as families cut down on shopping trips and saved more to see out the downturn. (page 7)

⇨ Four out of ten people in Britain have no pension provision whatsoever, according to a survey published today, as fears grow that an entire generation of workers faces poverty in retirement. (page 8)

⇨ Total UK personal debt at the end of June 2009 stood at £1,458bn. This has slowed further to 1.2% in the last 12 months which equates to an increase of ~£14.35bn (the increase was ~£116bn in January 2008). (page 9)

⇨ The highest levels of debt are in the south of England but the over-60s in Wales have one of the highest debt levels in the UK at £35,947. (page 10)

⇨ A life in debt reveals that Citizens Advice Bureaux debt clients owe an average of £16,971 – two-thirds more than in 2001, and the equivalent of almost 18 times their total monthly household income. It will take them an average of 93 years to pay off the money they owe at a rate they can afford. (page 11)

⇨ You can have a credit card from the age of 18. (page 14)

⇨ In just 12 months, 5.7 million people have received a boost to their credit card limit without their consent whilst 3% have seen their spending power slashed. (page 15)

⇨ Four out of ten consumers say they would rather pay for all transactions by card, according to research by payment solutions company RBS WorldPay. (page 15)

⇨ 71% of all cash acquired by consumers came from cash machines. 2.9 billion cash machine withdrawals were made in 2008 – equivalent to 91 withdrawals per second. (page 16)

⇨ In 1998, 80% of payments were made by cash, as opposed to 66% in 2008. (page 17)

⇨ If you are under 16 and working, you do not pay national insurance on your wages and will not have to pay income tax unless you earn over £4,195 a year. (page 20)

⇨ An impressive 86% of young people keep track of their money, up from 79% last year. (page 21)

⇨ Young people in the South West are best at budgeting with 89% keeping track of their money compared to 83% in the North East, North West and Scotland. (page 22)

⇨ Although there is no minimum legal age for someone to have a bank account, most banks offer basic accounts to young people aged 11 and over. (page 25)

⇨ Pre-paid cards are growing in popularity in the UK, and are particularly targeted at under-18s and people with a poor credit rating. Users load the pre-paid card with a certain amount of money, and can only spend what they have on the card – this means it is impossible to go overdrawn on a pre-paid card. (page 26)

⇨ Six out of ten university applicants from lower socio-economic backgrounds surveyed by the National Union of Students claimed that the recession had affected their choice of course or institution this year. The survey, published last month, shows that while 15% of all students surveyed chose universities where they could live at home, this was true of 27% of poorer students. (page 28)

⇨ The average expenditure of undergraduate students in their first year of study has increased by 12 per cent since 2004/05. This was driven by an increase of 68 per cent in the cost of participating in Higher Education – mainly due to the introduction of variable fees in 2006. (page 32)

⇨ An alarming 18.3% of 16 to 25 year olds are unemployed. (page 34)

⇨ In a Post Office survey, almost 60% of 18 to 24 year olds polled said they were living rent-free with their parents. (page 35)

⇨ A poll revealed over two-thirds of teenagers (70%) would like to be taught more about finance at school. (page 36)

⇨ A study in 2007 by one personal finance organisation found that half of young people were in debt by the age of 17 – a statistic that's even more alarming in view of the global credit crisis. (page 37)

# GLOSSARY

**Affluent**
Financially well-off.

**ATM**
Automated Teller Machine. Also called cash machines or, informally, the 'hole in the wall', these allow people to withdraw cash from their bank account using a cash card instead of going into their bank.

**Bank of England base rate**
The interest rate the Bank of England charges for secured overnight lending. It is used as a measure of the condition of the UK economy (a high rate represents a strong economy, a low rate can indicate a recession).

**The Budget**
The Budget is a statement made every year by the Government on where the money needed to spend on the country will come from, and what the money will be spent on. It's worked out by the Chancellor of the Exchequer with help from his office, the Treasury.

**Budgeting**
Budgeting is the art of keeping your spending under control through forward planning. It involves calculating in advance how much incoming cash you will have during a set period and how much you can therefore afford to spend in outgoings. You can then monitor your spending in various categories (food and drink, entertainment, travel etc.) and make sure you do not exceed the maximum amount you can afford to spend.

**Credit**
An amount of money added to an account. Also used in relation to borrowing: someone who is given approval to take out a loan, card or overdraft is said to have been given 'credit'.

**Credit crunch**
A reduction in the amount of credit available to people or a sudden difficulty in obtaining loans from banks. This can be a precursor to recession.

**Debit**
To transfer money out of an account in order to pay for a purchase or debt.

**Debt**
Money which is owed.

**Economy**
The way in which a region manages its resources. References to the 'national economy' indicate the financial situation of a country: how wealthy or prosperous it is.

**Expenditure**
The act of paying out money.

**Gross Domestic Product (GDP)**
The total value of the goods and services produced in a country within a year. This figure is used as a measure of a country's economic performance.

**Interest**
A fee charged on borrowed money. It is usually calculated as a percentage of the sum borrowed and paid in regular installments. An 'interest rate' refers to the amount of money charged on a borrowed amount over a given period. Interest can also be earned on money which is deposited in a bank account and is paid regularly by the bank to the account holder.

**Overdraft**
Someone is said to be 'overdrawn' if they have spent more than the amount of money they have in their bank account, giving a negative balance. An overdraft may be agreed in advance with the bank (authorised overdraft), meaning the account holder can withdraw up to the agreed amount without being penalised (they will usually be charged a set rate of interest for this privilege). However, becoming overdrawn without having previously agreed an overdraft with the bank can incur large fees.

**Pension**
Money paid to people after they have retired from work so they still have a regular income. A state pension is provided by the government after men have reached the age of 65 and women have reached 60. It is currently set at £95.20 a week. Many people will also contribute to a separate pension scheme during their working life which they can rely on in retirement.

**Recession**
A period during which economic activity has slowed, causing a reduction in Gross Domestic Product (GDP), employment, household incomes and business profits. If GDP shows a reduction over at least six months, a country is then said to be in recession. Recessions are caused by people spending less, businesses making less and banks being more reluctant to give people loans.

# INDEX

# Additional Resources

## Other Issues titles

If you are interested in researching further some of the issues raised in *Money and Finances*, you may like to read the following titles in the **Issues** series:

⇨ Vol. 181 *The Housing Issue* (ISBN 978 1 86168 505 6)

⇨ Vol. 167 *Our Human Rights* (ISBN 978 1 86168 471 4)

⇨ Vol. 160 *Poverty and Exclusion* (ISBN 978 1 86168 453 0)

⇨ Vol. 157 *The Problem of Globalisation* (ISBN 978 1 86168 444 8)

⇨ Vol. 154 *The Gender Gap* (ISBN 978 1 86168 441 7)

⇨ Vol. 149 *A Classless Society?* (ISBN 978 1 86168 422 6)

⇨ Vol. 139 *The Education Problem* (ISBN 978 1 86168 391 5)

⇨ Vol. 134 *Customers and Consumerism* (ISBN 978 1 86168 386 1)

⇨ Vol. 130 *Homelessness* (ISBN 978 1 86168 376 2)

⇨ Vol. 129 *Gambling Trends* (ISBN 978 1 86168 375 5)

⇨ Vol. 107 *Work Issues* (ISBN 978 1 86168 327 4)

For more information about these titles, visit our website at www.independence.co.uk/publicationslist

## Useful organisations

You may find the websites of the following organisations useful for further research:

⇨ **Abbey:** www.aboutabbey.com

⇨ **Aviva:** www.aviva.com

⇨ **Citizens Advice:** www.adviceguide.org.uk

⇨ **Consumer Credit Counselling Service:** www.cccs.co.uk

⇨ **Credit Action:** www.creditaction.org.uk

⇨ **Dept. for Work and Pensions:** www.dwp.gov.uk

⇨ **Joseph Rowntree Foundation:** www.jrf.org.uk

⇨ **Nationwide Education:** www.Nationwide Education.co.uk

⇨ **Need2know:** www.need2know.co.uk

⇨ **RBS Group:** www.moneysensepanel.co.uk

⇨ **Synovate:** www.synovate.com

⇨ **Talking Retail:** www.talkingretail.com

⇨ **TheSite:** www.thesite.org

⇨ **This is Money:** www.thisismoney.co.uk

⇨ **UK Payments Administration Ltd:** www.ukpayments.org.uk

⇨ **uSwitch:** www.uswitch.com

⇨ **Which?:** www.which.co.uk

⇨ **The World Bank:** http://youthink.worldbank.org

# ACKNOWLEDGEMENTS

The publisher is grateful for permission to reproduce the following material.

While every care has been taken to trace and acknowledge copyright, the publisher tenders its apology for any accidental infringement or where copyright has proved untraceable. The publisher would be pleased to come to a suitable arrangement in any such case with the rightful owner.

## Chapter One: The Economy

*The global financial crisis*, © International Bank for Reconstruction and Development, the World Bank, *Understanding the recession*, © TheSite, *How the credit crunch began*, © Which?, *The recession in numbers*, © Which?, *How to spot the end of a recession*, © Associated Newspapers Ltd, *Cost of living*, © Joseph Rowntree Foundation.

## Chapter Two: Managing Money

*Families cut spending by largest amount in decades*, © Telegraph Media Group Limited (2009), *It pays to save*, © Crown copyright is reproduced with the permission of Her Majesty's Stationery Office, *No pension plans for 40%*, © Guardian News & Media Ltd 2009, *Debt facts and figures*, © Credit Action, *Debt problems spread to the more affluent*, © Consumer Credit Counselling Service, *Research warns of deepening debt crisis*, © Citizens Advice, *Forms of payment*, © Nationwide Education, *Boosting credit card limits*, © uSwitch, *Cashless society favoured by four in ten shoppers*, © Talking Retail, *Report states that cash is still king, but for how long?*, © UK Payments Administration Ltd, *Women and financial independence*, © Synovate.

## Chapter Three: Young People's Money

*What age can I work?*, © CLIC, *Younger generation look to brighter financial futures*, © RBS Group, *Aviva identifies 'the forever generation'*, © Aviva, *The Budget 2009*, © need2know, *Banks and building societies*, © Hodder Murray 2009, *How to be a prudent student*, © Guardian News & Media Ltd 2009, *Budgeting*, © Credit Action, *Student income and expenditure 2007/08*, © Crown copyright is reproduced with the permission of Her Majesty's Stationery Office, *Young, jobless, broke: today's lost generation*, © Guardian News & Media Ltd 2009, *Two-thirds of teens demand better financial education*, © Abbey, *Money talks*, © Times Educational Supplement (TES).

## Photographs

**Flickr:** page 35 (Jason Cartwright).
**Stock Xchng:** pages 14 (Sophie); 16, 32 (Carl Silver); 21 (Carlos Zaragoza); 25 (Andy Culpin); 28 (hippihed); 36 (Kat Jackson).
**Wikimedia Commons:** page 2 (Mankind_2k).

## Illustrations

Pages 1, 6, 22, 33: Simon Kneebone; pages 3, 13, 24, 39: Don Hatcher; pages 5, 19, 27, 34: Angelo Madrid; pages 11, 29: Bev Aisbett.

And with thanks to the team: Mary Chapman, Sandra Dennis, Claire Owen and Jan Sunderland.

Lisa Firth
Cambridge
September, 2009